Southern Potteries Incorporated
Blue Ridge
Dinnerware

Revised 3rd Edition

By
Betty and Bill Newbound

Photos by Jimmy Tafoya

COLLECTOR BOOKS
A Division of Schroeder Publishing Co., Inc.

The current values in this book should be used only as a guide. They are not intended to set prices, which vary from one section of the country to another. Auction prices as well as dealer prices vary greatly and are affected by condition as well as demand. Neither the Authors nor the Publisher assumes responsibility for any losses that might be incurred as a result of consulting this guide.

On The Cover

Top: "Turkey with Acorns" platter, "Spring Bouquet" china demi pot.
Front: "Ida Rose" Sally shape jug, "Kaleidoscope" plate, "Spring Bouquet" china demi sugar and creamer.

Dedication

This book is dedicated to Norma, Sherman and Susan with much affection and gratitude, and to Aunt Florence, whose Easter tables set with Blue Ridge and love, started the whole thing so many years ago.

4

Acknowledgments and Thanks

As always, our heartfelt thanks to our readers; all those great Blue Ridge collectors who have written us about their finds and sent stacks of pictures and old advertisements. You have kept us informed on prices, related to us your memories of the old Southern Potteries heydays and even sent us your treasured pieces to photograph. How can we thank you enough? Without you, there would be no third edition.

Again, we thank our super photographer, Jimmy Tafoya, for coming out of retirement to give us the lovely pictures throughout the book. To our daughters, Laurie and Emalee, and our friend Nora Koch, publisher of *The Daze*, much love and appreciation for their continued support and encouragement.

Our gratitude to those who loaned parts of their collections for this edition and helped so much in other ways: Liz & Tom Newcomer, Kathryn & Lewis Lilley, Glenn Seabolt, Dick Brubaker, Rocky and Carol McReynolds, Julie Haben, Charles Huddleston, Ralph Grissom, Richard Freed and Joyce Crowson.

Finally, to our "Tennessee Connection," Norma and Sherman Lilly, and our "Atlanta Allies," Susan and Tom Moore, what can we say that is enough? For all your assistance, hard work and encouragement, and for your friendship, we thank you!!

Table of Contents

Prologue

Have eight years really gone by since our book was first published? Unbelievable! So many nice things are happening as "Blue Ridge Fever" sweeps the country. The Blue Ridge Collector's Club in Southern Potteries' hometown of Erwin, Tennessee, is sponsoring its 8th Annual Blue Ridge Show and Sale. The fascinating Unicoi Heritage Museum just outside Erwin has two rooms proudly featuring Blue Ridge. In nearby Blountville, Tennessee, we have the home of the National Blue Ridge Newsletter, which is doing so much to promote the hobby and to bring our "family" of collectors together. During recent years, several large China, Pottery and Glass Shows have featured Blue Ridge. There has evolved, among former pottery employees, an increased feeling of pride and accomplishment in the work they did. Somewhat to their own surprise, "those old dishes" they worked with for so many years have become valued collectors items – loved and cherished by people all over the country.

At this point, there seems to be a pattern emerging in collecting Blue Ridge. In rarity, the artist-signed pieces head the list, with the two large turkey platters, "Turkey Hen" and "Turkey Gobbler," proving to be the most elusive. The China Demi Pot which surfaced only recently, is considered very rare, with only a couple of examples known so far. The next hardest to find are Character Jugs with Paul Revere closely followed by the Indian. The five patterns made in the early 1950's to match Talisman Wallpaper may well turn out to be the rarest patterns in dinnerware, as the idea was not successful and few pieces were made. (See Talisman ads).

Most popular among collectors is the fascinating array of China pitchers, boxes, chocolate pots, vases, etc., produced in the mid-1940's. These are followed by the Christmas and Thanksgiving patterns and those depicting people, birds, fowl and farm or cabin scenes. Demi sets are popular, with the sugar and creamer seeming to be more elusive than the cups, saucers or teapot. Demi sets on their own trays are a real prize. Children's pieces, of course, are always loved and in demand.

The people we've met, the stories we've heard and especially the friends we've made, have been ample payment for the really demanding work involved in writing a book like this one. Aunt Florence's original set of Green Briar that started the whole thing – somewhat added to by this time – is now in our Emalee's apartment; still useful, still beautiful, still loved. And so, into yet another generation, the story goes on . . . . .

Introduction

When Bill and I were "going together" in the late 1940's, it was a family tradition to go to his Aunt Florence and Uncle Tom's for Easter dinner. I always looked forward to that because they were - and are - wonderful people. Aunt Florence was a great cook, and she loved to arrange her table so that dinner was a delight to the eye as well as the taste buds. Her dishes looked like Springtime itself; a gay, splashy pattern in shades of chartreuse and green and brown. I loved them! On the bottom of the plates was a mark showing a mountain and a pine tree and containing the words "Blue Ridge." I filed that information away in my mind.

After Bill and I were married, he had his army stint, and we spent a year and a half in Alaska. We had some dishes that came with the house we bought, but I didn't care much for them and when we came home again, the dishes stayed behind. After awhile, we got our home and the exciting time of furnishing it arrived. Naturally, one of the first things we needed was dishes, so we went downtown in Detroit to J.L. Hudson's. In those days when one looked for such a momentous item as one's first dinnerware, Hudson's was the place to go! When we arrived, I immediately thought of Aunt Florence and looked around for Blue Ridge. There it was - a gay, splashy display. Not too many patterns at that time, but all so pretty that it took us a long time to make our decision. Finally we decided on a cheerful floral design with one red flower, one yellow flower and green feathery looking trim on it's beaded edge. We didn't have a lot of money but found we could get a whole service for eight for about $20.00. Enough dishes to invite Aunt Florence and Uncle Tom to dinner too! Well, those dishes lasted and lasted. Sometimes we bought an extra piece or two to add to the set. Finally, by 1965, the cups gave out and I found to my distress that nobody carried them any more. At last, sadly, I packed the beloved Blue Ridge away. (After all, one doesn't just throw out an old friend!

"Gone but not forgotten" as the old saying goes, and years later when we got into the antique hobby, we found interesting pieces of Blue Ridge here and there; boxes, boots, eggcups, and we bought them, too. Now Blue Ridge is at last coming into it's own as a highly collectible item—all hand painted, no two pieces exactly alike. The beautiful work on many items, such as the signed turkey platters and the scenic plates, places them in the category of genuine Folk Art to be preserved and treasured in this age of mechanization, speed and sameness. No one with a wall full of Blue Ridge plates or a cabinet full of Blue Ridge pitchers and teapots can stay sad or downcast for long! We guarantee this hobby - and hopefully this book - will brighten your lives as it has our. Thanks, Aunt Florence!

History - Southern Potteries

Erwin, Tennessee, at the turn of the century was a typical, small Southern town, going on about its quiet existence. In just a few brief years, however, events began to take shape that were destined to change the town and its inhabitants immensely. The desire of the Carolina Clinchfield and Ohio Railroad to promote industry along its lines was the catalyst. Since the white Kaolin clay and Feldspar so necessary to pottery-making was available close to Erwin, land was purchased from the railroad's Holston Corporation for the purpose of building a pottery works. The pottery itself and about 40 company houses for rental to pottery workers were built on this land. The original pottery works consisted of one long building with seven "bee hive" type kilns; four for glaze and decorator firing, and three for bisque firing. All the kilns were coal-fired in the beginning. During the course of its history, the plant was enlarged and changed many times, with additional kilns being added in 1923. Eventually the coal-burning kilns were replaced with modern, oil-fired continuous tunnel kilns. In 1917, the town's inhabitants turned out at the railraod station to welcome several dozen skilled pottery tradesmen and their families imported from the areas of East Liverpool and Sebring, Ohio, and Chester, Virginia. Some manufacturing began at Erwin this year, mainly in traditional decal and gold-trimmed dinnerware, with the new company generally known as Clinchfield Pottery.

Southern Potteries Incorporated was issued a charter on April 8, 1920; the President and Vice-President being E.J. Owens and his son, Ted, from Minerva, Ohio, where Mr. Owens had been associated with Owens China Company. After a couple of mildly successful years, the Erwin plant was purchased by Charles W. Foreman, who had been associated with Owens in the aforementioned Owens China Company. George F. Brandt, another of Mr. Foreman's Ohio associates, was brought to Erwin as plant manager.

Mr. Foreman revolutionized Southern Potteries by bringing with him the technique of hand painting under glaze. This decoration was done mainly freehand by applying a metallic base color with sponge or brush to the bisque ware before glazing. Girls and women from the hills were trained in the freehand painting, and the quality of workmanship improved constantly until the gay, colorful ware we are familiar with was achieved. About 1938, Southern Potteries had evolved to full hand painting and Blue Ridge "Hand Painted Under The Glaze" dinnerware was born. Coming as it did into a dinnerware world of mainly decal type decorations with their necessarily rigid and uniform styling, Blue Ridge's fresh, uninhibited approach to design and their spectrum of vivid colors was a welcome innovation and an instant success. A large national sales organization was maintained, with eleven showrooms in carefully chosen cities, including Chicago's Merchandise Mart and an exclusive Fifth Avenue location in New York City. This organization, plus extensive advertising, made Blue Ridge one of the nation's leading dishware lines for many years. Oddly enough, there were no catalogs issued and very little information found its way into the trade journals.

Prior to World War II, the pottery industry in the United States was relatively small and struggling with the main bulk of dinnerware being imported. With the onset of the war, imports were cut off and United States potteries expanded enormously. Employment at Southern Potteries increased from about 100 in the beginning to over 1,000 during the peak production years of the mid 1940's and early 1950's. Most of the employees were in the hand-painting departments.

By 1953-1954, however, imports were again booming. Hard, unbreakable plastic dinnerware came onto the market very heavily and competition from other potteries was fierce. Labor costs were rising. The pottery business in this country was slackening, and Southern Potteries found itself dipping into its reserves in order to stay afloat. Rather than lay off employees, the plant went on half-time production. By late 1956, employment had dropped to something over 600 and production had been on a part-time basis for over a year.

On Thursday, January 31, 1957, an *Erwin Record* extra edition headlined "Southern Potteries Stockholders Vote to Close Plant." The action was not taken because of bankruptcy. Many potteries fell by the wayside during the late 1950's. Southern was one of the few that had anything left to liquidate. Remaining stockholders were paid approximately $7.50 per share upon closing. Large mail-order houses and trading-stamp premium firms were given the opportunity to stock up on patterns currently being offered in their catalogs. Mold cases (the master forms from which molds are made) were sold. Many of these were purchsed by Ray and Pauline Cash, owners of Clinchfield Artware Pottery and are still in use in the Cash family pottery currently operating in Erwin.

Southern Potteries' liquidation marked the end of over 40 years production of one of the nation's most attractive and original dinnerware. Shortly after the closing, the building was purchased by the National Casket Company, who made extensive alterations, leaving only the central core intact. The workers houses have long since been sold to individuals, and blended into the structure of the town. Although Southern Potteries is gone, memories of the "glory days," when it was one of the best in the nation, remain in the minds and hearts of the many original employees who still make their homes in and around Erwin.

8

The Potters

Picture a huge, sprawling white building with several projections and rooflines, covering 195,000 square feet of floor space and set near a wooded area in a small Southern town. Inside is a beehive of activity. Scores of potters' wheels for flatware are there; a casting department for holloware, a finishing department, a stamping department, five huge tunnel kilns and a sawtoothed-roof decorating shop. All this plus a barrel-making section (most china was shipped in barrels in the early days), and a section where the frit or glaze was made. Southern Potteries made their own saggers too in those earlier days. (A sagger is the ceramic box in which glazed ware is fired.) Add to this the mold storage area, the shipping department, the warehouse and the department that processed the basic raw materials used to make the clay bodies. Also there were the usual executive, clerical, sales and bookkeeping departments. Put them all together and you will have a picture of Southern Potteries in its heyday. In 1951, Southern Potteries was considered the largest hand-painting pottery in the United States, producing 24 million pieces a year and having over 1,000 employees, 40 percent of which were decorators. Southern Potteries was a union shop, but not closed. The National Brotherhood of Operative Potters (AFL) kept the pottery humming seven days a week, 24 hours a day.

The steps in making Blue Ridge dinnerware sound relatively simple, but great attention was paid to every detail to be sure of obtaining a top quality product. The raw materials used for the body - feldspar, flint, clays and talc - were first weighed and the correct proportions mixed for 40 minutes with water in a mixing machine. This made the slip. After several screening processes, some of the slip was routed to the slipcasting department, while the balance was pumped into filter presses which removed most of the water, resulting in what was called a "press cake." After a period of time, the press cake was again mixed with water and put into another machine which extruded the clay into a six-inch diameter column. This column was wire-cut into three-foot lengths and then de-aired. Sections of this prepared clay were then used for production material. The clay was processed in two ways: casting for holloware and jiggering for flatware.

Shaping flatware on a jigger or potter's wheel is known as "jiggering." A piece of clay is cut from the column and placed on the horizontal revolving wheel. This wheel shapes only the top side of the piece. The jiggerman shapes the bottom surface by using a hinged metal profiling tool. After the flatware piece has been formed, it goes on a trip through a dryer and then is smoothed by a finisher who wipes each piece with a wet sponge. Pieces are then dried overnight. Pipes carrying waste kiln gasses travel under the drying racks for heat.

A slightly different method is used for "jiggering" cups. A ball of clay is put into a mold which shapes the outside. At the same time, the jiggerman uses a hand tool which shapes the inside of the cup. "Turners" then trim the top edge of the cup with a knife and cut in the foot on which the cup stands. The turner then smooths the cup with a wet sponge and the handles which have been cast in a gang mold are pressed into place. After drying, the pieces are ready for bisque firing.

In the case of holloware, liquid clay or slip is poured into plaster of paris molds. The plaster of paris absorbs the water from the slip and builds up a layer of clay on the inside of the mold. When the desired thickness is achieved, the excess slip is poured out, dumped back into the mixers and re-used. After more drying, the mold is opened and the piece removed and allowed to air dry. At this point, the piece is tough and leathery and small cracks can be repaired. Excess material on mold edges is pared off with a knife and pieces are smoothed with a wet sponge before firing.

Imagine if you can, huge circular tunnel kilns up to 70 feet in diameter and holding up to 32 kiln cars, slowly revolving through their firing cycles. At temperatures up to 2000°F., the kiln cycle is 50-54 hours. The 65 foot long pusher kiln has an 18 hour cycle. Temperatures during firing were very closely watched with the help of ceramic pyrometric cones placed at intervals along the kiln. Excessive temperature could cause color changes or glaze difficulties.

After the initial firing, pieces were stamped, wax was applied to the foot of holloware pieces to prevent sticking, and the pieces went to the decorating shop. After being decorated, the glaze was applied. Holloware pieces were dipped, flatware was sprayed. A wet sponge was again used to wipe glaze off the areas which might touch. Flatware was placed in sagger boxes for firing. These were terra cotta boxes shaped to fit the pieces being fired. Triangle-shaped ceramic pins were inserted at intervals through the sides of the sagger, usually three pins to a piece, with the piece touching only the pointed edge of the pins. Small protrusions would result at the spots where the pieces touched the pins. Now pieces were ready for the second firing.

After being fired and cooled, the dinnerware was sent to a finishing department where any protrusions were knocked off with a piece of steel held in the hand. "You'd better have something over your eyes when walking through," a former employee told us. "You'd be cut by all that flying glass." The glaze, you see, actually does turn to glass after being fired.

Dinnerware was then sorted by comparing the finished product with perfect samples mounted on wall boards. Sorting was done according to pattern and quality of decorating. Also, any defective pieces were sorted out at this time. Even though Southern Potteries had outlets for seconds and sometimes even third quality pieces, there was still a certain amount of dinnerware that went to the dump behind the factory. The driver of the dump truck carried a baseball bat or some such implement and was supposed to break any pieces that were left whole after being dumped. Sometimes, however, he would be met by townspeople who asked him to "dump it gently" and he would "forget" to break pieces up. Then the folks would search through for usable pieces and take them home. Even to this day, the dumping spot is colorful with bits of china still bravely showing their bright flowers twenty-two years after the driver dumped that last truck-load of china.

In the early years, Blue Ridge was shipped mainly in barrels which were put together on the premises. Later, sets were packed in straw or in sectioned paper containers. Whichever method was used, some 425,000 pieces a week went on their way to major department stores and other retail outlets all across the country, making Blue Ridge America's leading hand-painted dinnerware.

The Decorators

"The dish rattling was terrific," a former Southern Potteries employee told us. Imagine 500 girls clashing dishes together, talking and laughing all in one huge, bright room! For the first years of Southern Potteries' life in Erwin, decal trimming was in use. Girls and women came from the hills and were trained in lining techniques during classes held on the second floor of the A.R. Brown & Company store building in downtown Erwin. Later, when complete hand painting had taken over, "on-the-job training" was used. The decorating shop foreman was very artistic. He would take a group of new girls into a section of the decorating room and teach them the basic folk painting strokes, working on broken pieces of china. After a few hours, they were given simple patterns to copy and often started work later the same day, filling in minor details in the patterns such as stems and leaves. As they gained more experience and became able, they were promoted to advanced work. Decorators worked in "crews" of two to four girls; one girl doing perhaps stems, one leaves, one petals, etc., depending on the intricacy of the pattern. Very difficult patterns sometimes had stamped guides that burned off during the final firing, but most patterns were purely free hand, copying from a master pattern piece. To keep the work from becoming too monotonous, patterns and jobs were changed frequently. The most talented painters graduated to decorating the chinaware items, where each girl painted an entire piece from start to finish.

Almost all the hundreds of patterns used originated at the plant. The chief designer, Lena Watts, was a native of Erwin. She was not a professional artist—just a girl with a flair for design, a feeling for color, and a love of nature. Her scenic plates depicting lonely cabins, mills and farm scenes, her various wildlife scenes and her huge turkey platters are indeed fine examples of folk art. In later years, Lena moved over to Stetson China Company, which explains the similarity between some Stetson patterns and Blue Ridge. Often buyers for the country's leading department stores would work with the decorators at Southern Potteries designing their own exclusive patterns. Buyers looked upon a trip to Erwin as a welcome change of pace and often stayed at the Hotel Erwin, which was reported to have excellent food and a resort atmosphere. Special order patterns such as these designer exclusives could be shipped within 30 days.

Colors were very important in the manufacture of Blue Ridge. Comprehensive studies were made of consumer likes and dislikes. If a certain color was popular, in say women's wear, it was likely to be popular in dinnerware also. Obtaining these exact colors and getting them to fire properly was a big problem. Pigments were purchased from as many as seven different color houses and were blended to obtain the desired shades. Large mail-order houses such as Sears Roebuck & Company often specified use of their own colors on exclusively designed dinnerware. By the end of World War II, 324,000 pieces of decorated ware were being turned out each week.

Put three or four plates of the same Blue Ridge pattern on your table together. Look at them carefully and see how many variations you can find in the pattern—a leaf here, a petal there, perhaps a flower added or left out, a vine tendril curling this way instead of that. There is an interesting old Pennsylvania Dutch story that was told in connection with the making of various types of fancy needlework. It was said that in each piece, the maker would be certain that there was at least one mistake, because if she did not, the perfect result would place her on the same level as God, which was of course unthinkable! Herein lies the charm of hand work, where each piece is different and where nothing is sterile and machine-perfect.

The huge decorating shop with its sawtooth roof has been torn down now, and the painters are gone. Nothing remains but the bright colored bits and pieces of china that still, after 22 years, litter the ground behind the factory building. But I think - if one listens very closely on a bright, still morning, you can hear the faint sound of dishes rattling . . . and laughter . . .

Shapes and Lines

Blue Ridge dinnerware is found in any of 11 different shapes or line treatments. They are:

Candlewick - beaded edge
Colonial - fluted shape
Skyline - sleek and plain
Trailway - wide painted borders
Astor - narrow, cupped rim
Rope Handle - holloware special

Piecrust - crimped edge
Clinchfield - wide, flat rim
Woodcrest - textured treatment
Monticello (Waffle) - border of
   incised squares
Moderne - futuristic, holloware only

The large, artist-signed turkey platters and scenic cabin and mill plates were done on the old Clinchfield shape, with the wide, flat rim, which was largely discontinued as a dinnerware shape when hand painting came into production. You will still find a few patterns in this shape.

Square shaped plates were mainly used as cake or salad plates and decorated to match whatever pattern the retailer selected. Other shapes you will occasionally find include "Rib," "Trellis," "Scalloped Beading" and "Lace Edge." These shapes were carried over from the old decal lines when hand painting first began. Also, bowls in odd shapes such as these were sometimes made for the premium trade, and did not come in complete dinnerware sets. Southern Potteries was very flexible as to production. If, for instance, a retailer ordered sets of Colonial dinnerware, but wanted a heavy rectangular tray or perhaps a pie baker to go with the set, Southern simply used plain, heavy blanks for these pieces, decorated them to match the pattern selected, and included them in the Colonial set.

Records are no longer available as to the exact dates of introduction of the various shapes. As far as we have been able to determine, Clinchfield was used in decal production and hand painting. The first three produced in all hand painting were Candlewick, Astor and Colonial. Advertisements show "the new" Piecrust shape in 1948 and Skyline in 1950. These were followed by Monticello, Woodcrest and Trailway. These last two used many of the Skyline blanks and were actually more a "line" or

"treatment" name rather than an actual shape name. In fact, Southern Potteries employees called Woodcrest by the name "Burlap" because the molds were actually lined with burlap to achieve the textured finish. Unfortunately, Woodcrest did not prove popular with the public and very little was made.

During the later years, trying valiantly to stay afloat in a disintegrating business climate, Southern introduced at least two lines of holloware designed to go with the simple, clean lines of the Skyline shape flatware. The so-called Moderne shape holloware pieces were made for a very short time. Along the same line of "anything for survival," Southern got rather heavily into the supermarket premium business. In order to change the product and differentiate between these supermarket patterns and their regular line, Southern introduced the Rope Handle holloware, again used with Skyline flatware. Boxed five-piece place settings of these patterns will sometimes be found. Generally the box will not mention Southern Potteries at all. The regular line of dinnerware never had separate boxed place settings; it was all sold either as open stock or packaged as complete sets.

Also during this time, a small line of ovenware was introduced. This included covered bowls, casseroles, batter sets, handled ramekins, pie bakers and rectangular baking dishes. Many of the pieces carried no mark at all or were simply marked "Oven Proof" in the familiar Southern Potteries script. Others used the regular ovenware backstamp illustrated in the chapter on marks.

CANDLEWICK: This is the "beaded edge" shape. Note the handles, also beaded. Shown in the "Delicious" pattern are the 9⅜" plate, 6" plate, gravy boat, 5¼" sauce, cup , saucer, covered sugar and creamer.

COLONIAL: The "fluted" shape. Note the graceful handles. Shown in the "Fruit Punch" pattern are the 9⅜" plate, 7" plate, 6" plate, cup saucer, 5¼" sauce, 9" round vegetable and 8" oval vegetable. Covered sugar and creamer are in the "Sunflower" pattern (C). Extra flat creamer is in the Fruit Fantasy pattern (B).

SKYLINE: This was the late, very streamlined shape. Shown are the 9″ round vegetable and covered sugar and creamer in "Streamers" pattern (C). The cup, saucer and coupe soup are in the "Weathervane" pattern (B). The shakers are in a "go with everything" red flower design. The ¼ lb. butterdish is in the "Chicken Pickins" pattern (B). This butterdish was painted to match many different patterns and was used with several different shapes as well.

PIECRUST: The popular shape with the crimped flange edge. Shown are the 9⅜″ plate, 6″ plate, 5¼″ sauce, gravy boat, cup, saucer, 6″ soup-cereal, 11½″ platter, 9″ round vegetable, covered sugar and creamer, all in the Green Briar pattern (B). Note: The sugar, creamer and gravy have approximately ½″ inward flanged edge.

ASTOR: This shape has a slightly cupped rim. Pictured is the "Valley Violet" breakfast set consisting of covered toast, butter pat, double eggcup, demi-pot, demi-sugar and creamer, regular size cup and saucer, 6″ plate, cereal bowl and 8½″ plate. Note: The breakfast set will be found in other patterns.

WOODCREST and RE-STYLED SKYLINE: These were late patterns and shapes not made in large quantities. Top row: "Eventide" plate, "Cactus" saucer, "Sweet Rocket" teapot in Woodcrest. Center: "Southern Rustic" saucer and cup in Re-Styled Skyline; "Eventide" cup and "Sunrise" sugar in Woodcrest. Foreground: Southern Rustic creamer and sugar in Re-Styled Skyline; "Sunrise" shakers in Woodcrest.

WAFFLE (sometimes called Monticello) and TRAILWAY: On the left we find blue bordered "Cassandra" pattern pieces in the Waffle edge; to the right are pieces of Cherokee Rose pattern in the Trailway holloware which were used with the Skyline flatware. "Cassandra" will also be found with a wine-red border.

PALISADES (1955-56): This was a very late holloware shape only, used with Skyline flatware. Top row, left to right: "Kimberly" 6" plate; "Grass Flower" bowl, "Shadow Fruit" jug. Center: "Kimberly" fruit; "Spiderweb" covered jug, "Kimberly" butter dish. Foreground: "Rosey" salt and pepper.

The revolving Lazy Susan, shown in the "Georgia" pattern was first pictured in a 1950 wholsesale catalog. Center bowl is 6¾" diameter. Outer pieces are 3⅞" wide, 1½" deep, 10" long "point to point." Base is blonde Birds-eye Maple, 20" diameter, 2¼" high. Mark on base is "G.H. Wood Products, Milwaukee, Wisconsin; G.H. Specialty Company."

Patterns

First of all, there were so many of them! At one point in its history, about 1951, Southern Potteries carried over 400 patterns in open stock. Some are intricate and beautiful; some are interestingly primitive and, let's face it, some are just plain awful! This variation is a part of the fascination of Blue Ridge collecting, because one never knows what will turn up.

The main bulk of Blue Ridge patterns were designed at the factory by a chief designer. Some patterns were designed by buyers from major department stores who worked with Southern Potteries' artists. Sometimes the painters themselves would change a pattern a bit perhaps by accident, perhaps on purpose—feeling they were improving it, or sometimes providing themselves a short-cut in their work. Lay three or four plates of the same pattern on the table and study them. Each one will be different—a leaf here, a blossom there—always some variation. In one large line, the plates were each made slightly different on purpose! Large retailers such as Sears Roebuck & Company often had patterns made exclusively for them and would become very upset if they found the same pattern on the market elsewhere, even after they had discontinued it themselves. To eliminate this problem, Southern Potteries would change the pattern slightly and return it to the market rather than scrap it entirely.

At first, our research indicated that when a certain pattern was found on a particular shape, that was it. However, more and more patterns have been turning up on two or more different shapes. This will necessitate mentioning the shape name as well as the pattern name when advertising to buy or sell by mail. We are also finding patterns with variations in edge or band coloring, such as "Arlene," which also comes with a yellow edge as well as the blue shown herein, and "Atlanta," which has been found with an added narrow black border. Near the end of Southern's production years, designs were stamped on the dinnerware with an intricately-made rubber stamp, and simply filled in by hand like a child's coloring book. Although many patterns were used in this "stamp and fill-in" method that are appealing to collectors today, this speed-up method of decorating was not well received at the time and was a contributing factor to the decline of Southern Potteries.

If you are accumulating a set, keep in mind that the smaller pieces such as cups, saucers, fruits, etc., often were decorated with only a part of the main pattern. For instance, if your pattern has a red and a blue flower on the dinner plate, a cup might have only the blue flower and the saucer only the red one.

We have learned that patterns were numbered more or less consecutively, so if you are lucky enough to find a plate or bowl with a number on it, you can very loosely date it by figuring that the three-thousand numbers were introduced in the 1940's and the four-thousand numbers in the 1950's. Each sample pattern was assigned a number, but many of them were never put into the line for various reasons. Too many brush strokes, too many colors, etc., might have made their manufacture too expensive. Also, patterns went "in" and "out" of fashion, due to style and colors used, just as most home furnishings do. Southern Potteries Marketing Departments kept a close eye on current home trends. Still, it is obvious that Southern Potteries produced a tremendous number of patterns! An interesting note is that the familiar "dot-dot-dot-dash" edge design found on many china pieces is the Morse Code signal for Victory, a wartime reminder.

Most Blue Ridge patterns were not named at the factory, only numbered. Occasionally when placing advertising in national magazines, the pottery would name the pattern shown therein. If the advertiser was a store, generally the store itself named the patterns in their ads. This fact has made it necessary for us to name the bulk of the patterns ourselves. If we could find advertised names, we used them. Also if we could find a name generally used by the decorators, we used it. All names enclosed by quotation marks indicate patterns named by us. Now and then, you will find a single pattern with two different names. Thankfully, this does not happen often, but when it does, it is usually caused by the "exclusive to area" agreement. This meant that Southern Potteries would sell a certain number of patterns to a store in, say, New York City. They would not sell these same patterns to any other store in the New York City area. However, they would sell the same patterns for instance, to a store in Dallas or perhaps Detroit. Sometimes it would happen that the New York store and the other store would both advertise the same pattern, each giving it a different name!

In the photo section to come, you will find the following information for each pattern: pattern name, shape name and pricing category "A-B-C". If you do not find your pattern in the pictures, check through the advertising reproduction section and perhaps you will find it there. Needless to say, all the patterns in the Blue Ridge dinnerware line were not available to us. The items shown do not, by any means, reflect Southern Potteries entire production. If you have patterns that we do not show, do write and tell us about them so that they may be included in a future update.

Photos include the author's collection plus pieces from the collections of many dedicated and helpful friends.

Top row, left to right: ''Alexandria,'' Candlewick, (B); ''Ledford,'' Candlewick, (B). Middle row, left to right: ''Heirloom,'' Candlewick, (B); ''Bristol Lily,'' Candlewick, (B). Bottom row, left to right: ''Brownie,'' Candlewick, (C); ''Brunswick,'' Candlewick, (B).

Top row, left to right: "Quaker Apple," Candlewick, (B); "Fayette Fruit," Candlewick, (B). Middle row, left to right: "Sundowner," Candlewick, (B); "Full Bloom," Candlewick, (B). Bottom row, left to right: "Spindrift," Candlewick, (C); "Confetti," Candlewick, (B).

Top row, left to right: ''Ham 'n Eggs,'' Candlewick, (B); ''Jan,'' Candlewick, (B). Middle row, left to right: Cock O' The Walk, Candlewick, (B); Grape Salad, Candlewick, (B). Bottom row, left to right: ''Sundance,'' Candlewick, (B); ''Sunshine,'' Candlewick, (C).

Top row, left to right: "California Poppy," Candlewick, (B); "Rooster Motto," Candlewick, (B); "Callaway," Piecrust, (B). Middle row, left to right: "Aurora," Candlewick, (B); "Glorious," Candlewick/Colonial, (B). Bottom row, left to right: "Rockport Rooster," Candlewick, (B); "Think Pink," Candlewick, (B).

Top row, left to right: "Tic Tack," Piecrust, (B); "Sampler," Piecrust, (B). Middle row, left to right: "Obion," Candlewick, (B); "Lenoir," Candlewick, (B). Bottom row, left to right: Mariner, Candlewick, (B); "Tulip Trio," Candlewick, (B). (This also found in blue, rose, yellow tulip combination known as "Multicolor Trio.")

Top row, left to right: "Magic Flower," Candlewick, (C); "Showgirl," Candlewick, (C). Middle row, left to right: "Betty," Candlewick, (C); "Dutch Iris," Candlewick, (B). Bottom row, left to right: "Carnival," Candlewick,(C); "Rose Red," Candlewick,(C).

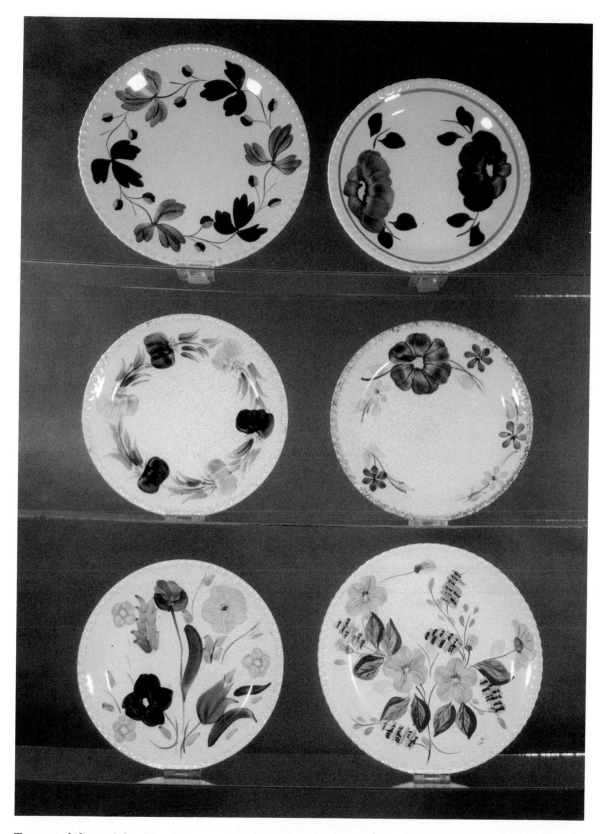

Top row, left to right: Mountain Ivy, Candlewick, (B); "Pom Pom," Candlewick, (C). Middle row, left to right: "Flower Wreath," Candlewick, (B); "Hilda," Candlewick, (C). Bottom row, left to right: "Mountain Nosegay," Candlewick/Astor, (B); "Country Garden," Candlewick, (B). Note: There is a "Pom Pom Variation" on the Colonial shape with no edge band and a three-two leaf combination.

Top row, left to right: ''Sweet Clover,'' Candlewick/Astor/Piecrust, (B). ''Yellow Poppy,'' Candlewick, (C). Middle row, left to right: ''Tuliptime,'' Candlewick, (C): ''Dutch Bouquet,'' Candlewick, (C). Bottom row, left to right: ''Appalachian Spring,'' Candlewick, (C); Smoky Mountain Laurel, Candlewick, (C).

Top row, left to right: Dahlia, Candlewick, (B); "Peony Bouquet," Candlewick, (C). Middle row, left to right: "Sungold #1," Candlewick, (C); "Bleeding Heart," Candlewick, (C). Bottom row, "Bluebell Bouquet," Candlewick, (B); also found with all green leaves.

Top row, left to right: "Plum Duff," Candlewick, (C); "Gooseberry," Candlewick, (C). Middle row, left to right: "Delicious," Candlewick, (B); "Blue Moon," Candlewick, (C). Bottom row, left to right: "Dutch Tulip," Candlewick, (C); "Gumdrop Tree," Candlewick, (C); "Spring Glory," Candlewick, (C).

Top row, left to right: Language of Flowers Cake or Salad pieces, #2, #3. Middle row, left to right: Language of Flowers #4, Candlewick, (B); Provincial Farm Scenes, 8″ plate, "Milkmaid." (These also in 6″ sq. plates and large serving plate.) Bottom row, left to right: "Tennille," Candlewick, (C), "Vibrant," Candlewick, (C).

Top row, left to right: "Stuck Up," Candlewick, (B); "Sarah," Candlewick, (C). Middle row, left to right: Highland Posy, Candlewick, (C); "Bracelet," Candlewick, (B). Bottom row, left to right: "Polly," Candlewick, (C); "Green Lanterns," Candlewick, (C).

Top row, left to right: "Rosemary," Candlewick, (B); Twin Flowers, Candlewick, (C). Middle row, left to right: "Louisiana Lace," Candlewick, (C); "Christmas Ornament," Candlewick, (B). Bottom row, left to right: "Mountain Rose," Candlewick, (C); "Vixen," Candlewick, (C).

Top row, left to right: "Amelia," Candlewick, (C); Lace & Lines, Candlewick, (C). Middle row, left to right: "Moccasin," Candlewick, (C); "Together," Candlewick, (C). Bottom row, left to right: "Fruit Medley," Candlewick, (B); "Courtland," Floral Point, (C).

Top row, left to right: "Anemone," Piecrust, (C); "Magnolia," Piecrust, (B). Middle row, left to right: "Wild Cherry #3," Piecrust, (C); "Ring-O-Roses," Piecrust, (B). Bottom row, left to right: "Daffodil," Piecrust, (B); "Della Robbia," Piecrust, (B).

Top row, left to right: Southern Camelia, Piecrust, (C); Green Briar, Piecrust, (B). Middle row, left to right: "Spray," Piecrust, (C); "Apple Crunch," Piecrust, (C). Bottom row, left to right: "Cantata," Piecrust, (B); Highland Ivy, Piecrust, (C).

Top row, left to right: "Cadenza," Piecrust, (B); "Flirt," Piecrust, (B). Middle row, left to right: "Jessamine," Piecrust, (B); "Whirligig," Piecrust, (B). Note: A Whirligig variation in colors of chartreuse and brown is called Bow Knot — also found on Colonial shape with all red buds and no edge decoration. Bottom row, left to right: "Tempo," Piecrust, (B); "Camelot," Piecrust, (B).

Top row, left to right: "Spring Morning," Piecrust, (B); "Kibler," Piecrust, (B). Middle row, left to right: Ridge Harvest, Piecrust, (B); "Cherry Wine," Piecrust, (B). Bottom row, left to right: "Cheers," square, (B); "Singing Rooster," square, (B); "Dream Girl," square, (B).

Top row, left to right: "Folklore," Woodcrest, (B); "Cherry Tree Glen," Piecrust, (B). Middle row, left to right: "Reflection," Piecrust, (B); "Floribunda," Piecrust, (B). Bottom row, left to right: "Aragon," Piecrust, (C); "Hillside," Piecrust, (B).

Top row, left to right: "Bouquet," Astor, (B); "Plume," Astor, (C). Middle row, left to right: "Sundrops," Astor, (C); "Waterlily," Astor, (B). Bottom row, left to right: "Flowering Berry," Candlewick, (B); "Red Tulip," Candlewick, (C).

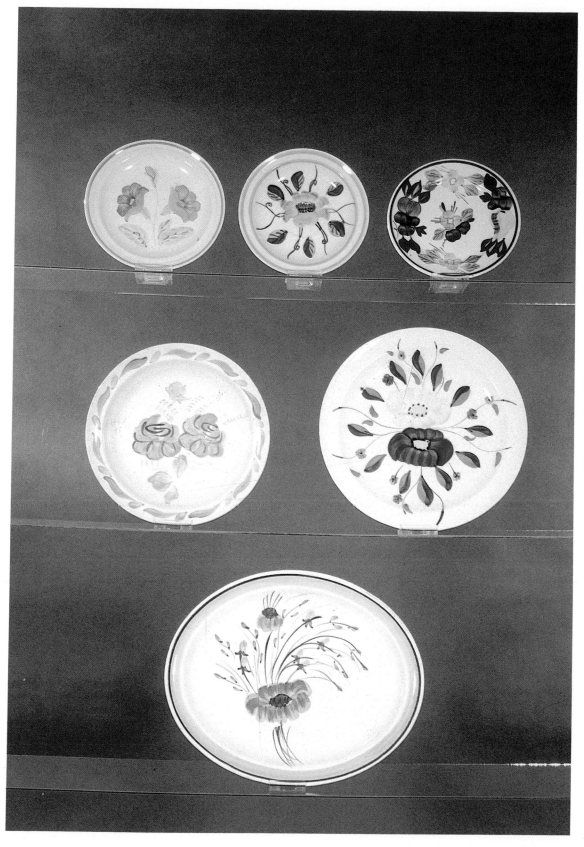

Top row, left to right: "Pastel Poppy," Astor, (B); "Periwinkle," Astor, (C); "Mary," Astor, (B). Middle row, left to right: "Corsage," Astor, (B); "Cumberland," Astor, (B). Bottom row: "Pauline," Astor, (B).

Top row, left to right: "Fairy Tale," Astor, (C); "Little Violet," Astor, (C). Middle row, left to right: "Hopscotch," Astor, (B); "Kingsport," Astor, (C). Bottom row, left to right: "Bristol Bouquet," Astor, (B); "Roanoke," Astor, (B).

Top row, left to right: "Jonquil," Astor, (B); "Memory Lane," Astor, (B). Middle row, left to right: "Kitchen Shelf," Astor, (B); "Fluffy Ruffles," Astor, (B). Bottom row, left to right: "Bellemeade," Astor, (B); "Concord," Astor, (B).

Top row, left to right; "Fetching," Astor, (B); "Threesome," Astor, (B). Middle row, left to right: "Beggarweed," Astor, (B); "English Garden," Astor, (B). Bottom row, left to right: "Beverly," Astor, (B); "Folk Art Fruit," Astor, (B).

Top row, left to right: "Yellow Ribbon," Astor, (B); "Lambkin," child's 8½", Astor. Middle row, left to right: "Roseanna," Astor, (B). Note: also found in teal colors and with varying edge borders; "Tennessee Waltz," Astor, (B). Bottom row, left to right: "Scattered Leaves," Astor, (B); "Bachelor Buttons," Astor, (B).

Top row, left to right: "Bug-A-Boo," Astor, (B); "Sonora," Astor, (B). Middle row, left to right: "Recollection," Astor, (B); "Tara," Astor, (B). Bottom row, left to right: "Blossom Time," Astor, (B), "Vineyard," Astor, (B).

Top row, left to right: "Indian Summer," Astor, (B). "Pink Lady," Astor, (B). Middle row, left to right: "Golden Jubilee," Astor, (B); "Spring Shower," Astor, (B). Bottom row, left to right: "Mod Apple," Square, (C); Darcy, Square, (B).

Top row, left to right: "Dragon Song," Astor, (B); "Fanciful," Clinchfield (B). Middle row, left to right: "Abracadabra," Clinchfield, (B); "Mosaic," Clinchfield, (B). Bottom row, left to right: "Kaleidoscope," Clinchfield, (B). These first five plates are known as Designer Plates and were not put into the general line. How many were made is a mystery. #8 Astor Songbird plate. (B).

Top row, left to right: "Bridesmaid," Clinchfield, (B); "Baby Doll," Clinchfield, (B); "Red Letter Day," Clinchfield, (B). Middle row, left to right: "Clinging Vine," Clinchfield, (B); Tulip Row, Clinchfield, (B). Bottom row, left to right: "Flamboyant," Clinchfield, (B); "Fern," Clinchfield, (B).

Top row, left to right: "Winner's Circle," Clinchfield, (B); "Blackberry," Clinchfield, (B). Middle row, left to right: "Game Cock," Clinchfield, (B); "Winery," Clinchfield, (B). Bottom row, left to right: "Tulip Circle," Clinchfield, (B); "Prima Donna," Clinchfield.

Top row, left to right: "Lyonnaise," Man and Woman, Clinchfield, (B). Middle row, left to right: "Beauty Secret," Clinchfield, (B); "Freedom Ring," Astor, (B). Bottom row, left to right: "Pansy," Clinchfield, (B); "Flowry Branch," Astor, (B).

Top row, left to right: "Windjammer," Clinchfield, (B); "Cocky-Locky," Clinchfield, (B). Middle row, left to right: "Love Song," Astor, (B); "Picardy," Clinchfield, (B). Bottom row, left to right: "Eglantine," Clinchfield, (B); "Calais," Astor, (B); "Primrose Path," Astor (B).

Top row, left to right: "Veronica," Clinchfield, (B); "Brittany," Clinchfield, (B). Middle row, left to right: "Unicoi," Clinchfield, (B); "Red Queen," Clinchfield, (B). Bottom row, left to right: "Fairmede Fruits," Clinchfield, (B); "Ruby," Clinchfield, (B).

Top row, left to right: Clover, Clinchfield, (C); "Cattails," Trailway, (C). Middle row, left to right: "Gingham Fruit," Trailway (C); "Hawaiian Fruit," Clinchfield/Piecrust, (B). Bottom row, left to right: "Red Cone Flower," Clinchfield, (C); "Pricilla," Clinchfield, (B).

Top row, left to right: ''Gingham Fruit,'' Trailway, (B); ''Cock-a-Doodle,'' Skyline, (B). Middle row, left to right: ''Country Fruit,'' Trailway, (B); ''Thistle,'' Trailway, (B). Bottom row, left to right: ''Leaves of Fall,'' Trailway, (B); ''Fruit Ring,'' Clinchfield, (B).

Top row: "Ming Tree," Woodcrest, (B). Middle row, left to right: "Quilted Ivy," Woodcrest, (C); "June Apple," Woodcrest (C). Bottom row, left to right: Eventide, Woodcrest, (B); "Bamboo," Woodcrest, (C).

Top row: ''Belle Haven,'' Woodcrest, (B). Middle row, left to right: ''Sweet Rocket,'' Woodcrest, (B); ''Maple Leaf,'' Woodcrest, (C). Bottom row, left to right: ''Caretta Cattail,'' Woodcrest, (C); ''Ming Blossom,'' Woodcrest, (C).

Top row, left to right: Stencil, Woodcrest, (C); "Exotic," Woodcrest, (B). Middle row, left to right: "Pleasant Acres," Woodcrest, (B); "Quilted Fruit," Woodcrest, (B). Bottom row, left to right: "Apple-yard," Woodcrest, (B); "Aqua Leaf," Woodcrest, (C).

Top row, left to right: "Cosmos," Skyline, (C); "Cheerio," Skyline, (B). Middle row, left to right: "Fantasia," Skyline, (B); "Tropical," Skyline, (B). Bottom row, left to right: "Night Flower," Skyline, (B); "Mountain Sweetbriar," Skyline, (C).

Top row, left to right; "Wild Cherry #1," Skyline, (C); "Atlanta," Moderne, (C). (Also found with narrow black band edge.) Middle row, left to right: "Mayflower," Skyline, (C). (Also found on blue stippled background.) "Desert Flower," Skyline, (B). Bottom row, left to right: "Pinkie," Skyline, (C); "Wild Cherry #2," Skyline, (C).

Top row, left to right: "Red Barn," Skyline (also found on white background); Weathervane, Skyline. Middle row, left to right: "Chicken Pickins," Skyline; "Cock 'O The Morn," Skyline. Bottom row, left to right; "Chanticleer," Skyline, "Pink Dogwood," Palisades. Note: "Cock 'O The Morn" also found on Woodcrest with white background.

Top row, left to right: Plantation Ivy, Skyline, (C); "Rock Garden," Skyline, (D). Middle row, left to right: "Tuna Salad," Skyline, (C); "Calico Farm," Skyline (B). Bottom row, left to right: "Stanhome Ivy," Skyline, (C); "Autumn Breeze," Skyline, (C).

Top row, left to right: "Harvestime," Moderne (C); "Winesap," Skyline, (C). Middle row, left to right: "Pippin," (Also known as Valencia), Skyline, (C); "Bittersweet," Skyline (C). Bottom row, left to right: "Fantasy Apple," Skyline, (C); "Apple Jack," Skyline, (B).

Top row, left to right: "Rustic Plaid," Skyline, (C); "Festive," Skyline, (C). Middle row, left to right: "Ribbon Plaid," Skyline, (C); "Basketweave," Skyline, (C). Bottom row, left to right: "Spiderweb," Skyline, (C); "Silhouette," Skyline, (C). (Spiderweb and Silhouette will be found in other colors.) Note: "Spiderweb" also found in blue and yellow.

Top row, left to right: "Partridge Berry," Skyline, (C); "Sonata," Skyline, (C). Middle row, left to right: "Garden Pinks," Skyline, (C); "Columbine," Skyline, (C); "Green Eyes," Skyline, (C). Bottom row, left to right: Evening Flower, Skyline, (C); "Shadow Fruit," Skyline (C). Note: Also found with pink/charcoal line edge.

Top row: "Normandy," Skyline, (B); (man and woman in set). Middle row, left to right: "Frageria," Skyline, (B); "Granny Smith Apple," Skyline, (B). Bottom row, left to right: "Black Ming," Skyline, (C); "Razzle Dazzle," Skyline, (B). Note: "Black Ming" also found on Woodcrest shape.

Top row, left to right: ''Falmouth,'' Skyline, (B); ''Chicken Feed,'' Skyline, (B). Middle row, left to right: ''Bardstown,'' Skyline, (B); ''Pinecone,'' Skyline, (B). Bottom row, left to right: ''Bonsai,'' Skyline, (B); ''Meadowlea,'' Skyline, (B).

Top row, left to right: "Violet Spray," Skyline, (B); Forest Fruit, Skyline, (B). Middle row, left to right: "Greensville," Skyline, (B); "Southern Dogwood," Skyline, (B). Bottom row, left to right: "Foxfire," Skyline, (B); "Gaiety," Skyline, (B) — also found with yellow flowers and brown centers with small leaves.

Top row, left to right: "Soddy-Daisy," Skyline, (B); "Winnie," Skyline, (B). Middle row, left to right: "Wheat," Skyline, (C); "Dandridge Dogwood," Skyline, (C). Bottom row, left to right: "Jellico," Skyline, (B); "Queen Ann's Lace," Skyline, (B).

Top row, left to right: "Wishing Well," Skyline, (B); "Red Rooster," Skyline, (B). Middle row, left to right: "Gloriosa," Skyline, (B); "Berry Patch," Skyline, (B). Bottom row, left to right: "Rockcastle," Skyline, (B); "Homestead," Skyline, (B).

Top row, left to right: "Vegetable Patch," Skyline, (B); "Farmyard," Skyline, (B). Middle row, left to right: "Pilgrims," Skyline, (B); "Flight," (C). Bottom row, left to right: "Fireside," Skyline, (B); "Homeplace," Skyline. (B). Note: "Vegetable Patch" various size plates will have a different vegetable.

Top row, left to right: "Caroline," Skyline, (C), (also found on Woodcrest). "Fairmont," Skyline, (B), (cups solid brown). Middle row, left to right: "Susan," Skyline, (B); "Aloaha," Skyline, (B). Bottom row, left to right: "Patricia," Skyline, (B); "Floweret," Skyline, (B).

Top row, left to right: "Lavalette," Palisades; "Bethany Berry," Palisades. Middle row, left to right: "Strawberry Sundae," Skyline; "Jigsaw," Skyline. Bottom row, left to right: "Christmas Doorway," Skyline; Feathered Friends," Skyline. Note: "Strawberry Sundae" also found on Colonial blank.

Top row: "Veggie," Skyline, (B), Pair of snack plates with cup well. Middle row, left to right: "Arlington Apple," Skyline, (B); "Apple Crisp," Skyline, (B). Bottom row, left to right: "Squares," Skyline, (C); Blossom Tree, Skyline, (B), "Blue Willow," Trellis, (C). Note: Blossom Tree is a Talisman Wallpaper pattern.

Top row, left to right: ''Briarwood,'' Skyline, (C); ''Tea Rose,'' Skyline, (B). Middle row, left to right: ''Midas Touch,'' Skyline, (B) ''Windmill,'' Skyline, (B). Bottom row, left to right: ''Chloe,'' Skyline, (C); ''Spring Mills,'' Skyline, (C).

Top row, left to right: Medallion, Skyline, (B); "Peggy," Skyline, (C). Middle row, left to right: "Sandra," Skyline, (C); "Pippa," Skyline. (B). Bottom row, left to right: "French Knots," Skyline, (C); "Loretta," Skyline, (C).

Top row, left to right: "Japanese Wallflower," Skyline, (C); "Cecilia," Skyline, (B). Middle row, left to right: "Double Cherry," Skyline, (C); "Fruit Crunch," Skyline, (B). Bottom row, left to right: "Wild Geranium," Skyline, (B); "Sweet Sue," Skyline, (B).

Top row, left to right: "Lacey," Skyline, (C); Hops, Skyline, (C). Middle row, left to right: "Kismet," Skyline, (C); "Upstart," Skyline, (C). Bottom row, left to right: "Mountain Strawberry," Skyline, (C); "Wintertime," Skyline, (C).

Top row, left to right: "Hopewell," Skyline, (C); "Anjou," Skyline, (B). Middle row, left to right: "John's Plaid," Skyline, (C); Sunny Spray, Skyline, (B). Bottom row, left to right; "Mayflower With Blue," Skyline, (C); "Bonaire," Skyline, (C).

Top row, left to right: "Turkey with Acorns," Skyline/Clinchfield, (B). Middle row, left to right: "Thanksgiving Turkey," Skyline/Clinchfield, (B); Petal Point, Skyline, (B). Bottom row, left to right: Lotus, Skyline, (C); "Homeplace," Skyline, (B). Note: cups and saucers of both turkey patterns have edge designs only.

Top row: "Deep Purple," square cake plate, (B). Middle row, left to right: "Arlene," Trellis, (B); "Antique Leaf," Lace Edge, (C). Bottom row, left to right: "Oriental Poppy," Colonial, (B); "Wild Irish Rose," Colonial, (B). Note: "Arlene" found also with yellow border. "Antique Leaf" also yellow/green/black, pink/blue/green, red/blue/yellow, and all red leaves.

Top row, left to right: "Tiger Lily," Colonial, (B); "Garland," Colonial, (B). Middle row, left to right: "Norma," Colonial, (B); "Zinnia," Colonial, (B). Bottom row, left to right: "Petunia," Colonial, (B); "Flower Ring," Colonial, (B). Note: "Petunia" also found marked Laurel Wreath and Collete on Candlewick blanks.

Top row, left to right: "Blue Heaven," Colonial, (B); "Penny Serenade," Colonial, (C). Middle row, left to right: "Grandmother's Garden," Colonial/Astor, (B); "Chintz," Colonial, (B). Bottom row, left to right: "Chrysanthemum," Colonial, (C); "Sweet Pea," Colonial (B).

Top row, left to right: "Patchwork Posy," Colonial, (C); "Calico," Colonial, (B). Middle row, left to right: "Painted Daisy," Colonial, (B); "Symphony," Colonial, (C). Bottom row, left to right: "Sherry," Colonial, (B); "Falling Leaves," Colonial/Astor, (B).

Top row: "Big Apple," Colonial, (B). Middle row, left to right: "Crab Apple," Colonial, (B); "Beaded Apple," Colonial, (C). Bottom row, left to right: "Cherry Coke," Colonial, (C); "Autumn Apple," Colonial, (B). Note: "Crab Apple" also found with two and one apples.

Top row: "Peony," Colonial. Middle row, left to right: "Laurie," Colonial, (B); "Chickory," Colonial, (B). Bottom row, left to right: "Daydream," Colonial, (C); "Coreopsis," Colonial, (C). Note: "Peony" also found marked Camelia, Blue Ridge Mountain Hand Art.

Top row, left to right: "Orchard Glory," Colonial, (C); "Fruit Punch," Colonial (B). Middle row, left to right: Fruit Fantasy, Colonial (B); "Bountiful," Colonial, (B). Bottom row, left to right: "Wild Strawberry," Colonial, (C); "Strawberry Patch" Colonial, (B).

Top row, left to right: "Rugosa," Colonial, (B); "Sungold #2," Colonial, (C). Middle row, left to right: "Bridal Bouquet," Colonial, (B); "Rosalinde," Colonial, (B). Bottom row, left to right: "Wild Rose," Colonial, (B); "June Bouquet," Colonial (B).

Top row, left to right: ''Paper Roses,'' Colonial, (B); ''June Rose,'' Colonial, (B). Middle row, left to right: ''Mountain Bells,'' Colonial, (C); ''Mod Tulip,'' Colonial, (C). Bottom row, left to right: ''Sunny,'' Colonial, (C); ''Shoo Fly,'' Colonial, (C).

Top row, left to right: "Susannah," Colonial, (C); "Meadow Beauty," Colonial, (C). Middle row, left to right: "Hollyhock," Colonial, (B); "Field Daisy," Colonial, (B). Bottom row, left to right: "Dream Flower," Colonial, (B); "Gypsy," Colonial, (B).

Top row, left to right: "Christmas Tree," Colonial/Skyline, (B); "Mickey," Colonial, (B). Middle row, left to right: "Waltz Time," Colonial, (B); "Mountain Aster," Colonial (B). Bottom row, left to right: "French Peasant," Colonial, (B), Also with green/orange edge pattern. "Farmer Takes a Wife," Colonial, (B).

Top row, left to right: Mardi Gras, Colonial, (B); "Crocus," Colonial, (C). Middle row, left to right: "Cowslip," Colonial, (C); "Cherry Cobbler," Colonial (C). Bottom row, left to right: "Buttercup," Colonial, (C); "Fairy Bells" Colonial (C). Note: Mardi Gras also with blue trim and on Candlewick with red trim.

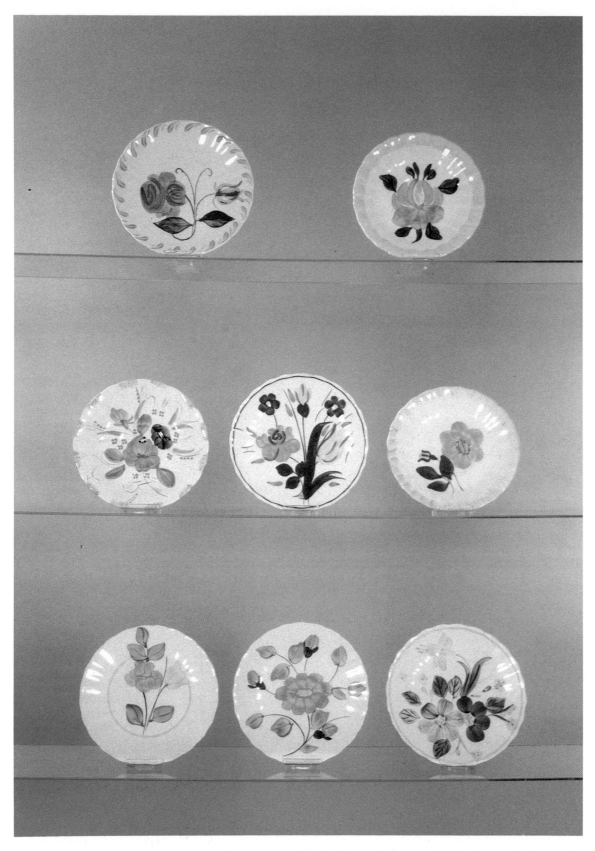

Top row, left to right: "Ridge Rose," Colonial, (B); "Delft Rose," Colonial, (C). Middle row, left to right: "Dresden Doll," Colonial (B); "Garden Lane," Colonial, (B); "Wrinkled Rose," Colonial, (C). Bottom row, left to right: "June Bride," Colonial, (C); "Rock Rose," Colonial, (C); "Rhapsody," Colonial, (B). Note: "Rock Rose" also found in yellow.

Top row, left to right: "Constance," Colonial, (B); "Mardi Gras Variant," Colonial, (B). Middle row, left to right: "Jessica," Colonial, (B); "Tanglewood," Colonial, (B). Bottom row, left to right; "Memphis," Colonial, (B); "Cinnabar," Colonial, (B).

Top row, left to right: "Abundance," Colonial, (B); "Fruit Sherbet," Colonial, (B). Middle row, left to right: "Bosc," Colonial, (C); "Vintage," Colonial, (B). Bottom row, left to right: "Colonial Birds #1 and #2," Colonial, (B).

Top row, left to right: "Fruit Salad," Colonial, (B); "Berryville," Colonial, (B). Middle row, left to right: "Hollyberry," Colonial, (B); "Roan Mountain Rose," Colonial, (B). Bottom row, left to right: "Lexington," Colonial, (C); "Orion," Colonial, (B). Also found in light blue.

Top row, left to right: "Edgemont," Colonial, (B); "Ashland," Colonial, (B). Middle row, left to right: "Joyce," Colonial, (B); "Flounce," Colonial, (B). Bottom row, left to right: "Red Willow," Colonial, (C); "North Star Cherry," Colonial, (B).

Top row, left to right: ''Verona,'' Colonial (B); ''Autumn Laurel,'' Colonial, (B). Middle row, left to right: ''Stardancer,'' Colonial, (B); ''Carlile,'' Colonial, (C). Bottom row, left to right: ''Polka Dot,'' Colonial, (B); ''Amarylis,'' Colonial, (B). Note: ''Polka Dot'' is one of the few patterns with flowers painted inside the cup.

Top row, left to right: "Becky," Colonial, (B); "Nocturne," Colonial, (B). Middle row, left to right: "Rainelle," Colonial, (B); "Pembrooke," Colonial, (B). Bottom row, left to right: "Sunbright," Colonial, (B); "Bluefield," Colonial, (B).

Top row, left to right: Fox Grape, Colonial, (B); "Rose Hill," Colonial, (B). Middle row, left to right: "Snappy" Colonial, (B); "Clairborne," Colonial, (B). Bottom row, left to right: Yorktown, Colonial, (B); "Blue Flower," Colonial, (C). Note: Yorktown is a Talisman Wallpaper pattern.

Top row, left to right: "Karen," Colonial, (B); "Laura," Colonial, (B). Middle row, left to right: "Wildwood," Colonial, (B); "Sarepta," Colonial, (B). Bottom row, left to right: "Breckenridge," Colonial, (B); "Strathmoor," Colonial, (B).

Top row, left to right: "Sunfire," Colonial, (B); "Meylinda," Colonial, (B). Middle row, left to right: "Briar Patch," Colonial, (B); "Country Road," Colonial, (B). Bottom row, left to right: "Pink Petticoat," Colonial, (B); "Amhurst," Colonial, (C). Note: "Country Road" also found without black specks in flower centers. (Guess the "bugs" left!), and also on Candlewick blank.

Top row, left to right: "Medley," Colonial, (B); "Kate," Colonial, (B). Middle row, left to right: "Champagne Pinks," Colonial, (B); "Hornbeak," Colonial, (B). Bottom row, left to right: "Potpourri," Colonial, (B); "Cherry Blossom," Colonial, (B).

Top row, left to right: "Colonial Rose," Colonial, (B); "Tazewell Tulip," Colonial, (B). Middle row, left to right: "Victoria," Colonial, (B); "Liz," Colonial, (B). Bottom row, left to right: "Blackberry Lily," Colonial, (B); "Gypsy Dancer," Colonial, (B).

Top row, left to right: ''Pandora,'' Colonial, (B); ''Spring Hill Tulip,'' Colonial, (B). Middle row, left to right: ''Blue Tango,'' Colonial, (B); ''Bramwell,'' Colonial, (B). Bottom row, left to right: ''Berea Blossom,'' Colonial, (B); Poinsetta, Colonial/Skyline, (B).

Top row, left to right: "County Fair," Colonial, (B); "Tickled Pink," Colonial, (B). Middle row, left to right: "Alleghany," Colonial, (B); "Pristine," Colonial, (B). Bottom row, left to right: "Flower Bowl," Colonial (B); "Joanna," Colonial, (B).

Top row, left to right: "Rutledge," Colonial, (B); "Fuchsia," Colonial, (B); "Manassas," Colonial, (B). Middle row, left to right: "Nadine," Colonial, (B); "Texas Rose," Candlewick, (B); "Barbara," Colonial, (B). Bottom row, left to right: "Color Stitch," Colonial, (C); "Bourbon Rose," Colonial, (B); "Rosette," Colonial, (B). Note: "Rosette" larger plates also have a pink flower.

Top row, left to right: "Lace-leaf Coreopsis," Colonial, (C); "Ruth Anna," Colonial, (B). Middle row, left to right: "Triple Treat," Colonial, (C); "Cordele," Colonial, (C). Bottom row, left to right: "Angelina," Colonial, (B); "Erwin Rose," Colonial, (B).

Top row, left to right: "Wildwood Flower," Colonial, (B); "Savannah," Colonial, (B). Middle row, left to right: "Roxalana," Colonial, (B); "Pansy Trio," Colonial, (B). Bottom row, left to right: "Wrinkled Rose," Colonial, (B); "Shenandoah," Colonial, (B).

Top row, left to right: "Lighthearted," Colonial, (B); "Oakdale," Colonial, (B). Middle row, left to right: "Flutter," Colonial, (B), "Rambling Rose," Colonial, (B). Bottom row, left to right: "Dazzle," Colonial, (B); Sun Bouquet, Colonial, (B).

Top row, left to right: "Teacher's Apple," Colonial, (C); "Exhuberant," Colonial, (B). Middle row, left to right: Violets, Colonial, (B); "Louisa," Colonial, (B). Bottom row, left to right: "Elizabeth," Colonial, (B); "Old Refrain," Colonial, (C).

Top row, left to right: Crab Apple (also see page 81), Colonial, (B); "Viola," Colonial, (B). Middle row, left to right: Ridge Daisy, Colonial, (B); "Apple Trio," Colonial, (C). Bottom row, left to right: "Cherry Drops," Colonial, (B); "Georgia Belle," Colonial, (C).

Top row, left to right: "Mirror Image," Colonial, (B); "Sunday Best," Colonial, (B). Middle row, left to right: "Show-Off," Colonial, (C); "Rambling Rose," Colonial, (C). Bottom row, left to right: "Cherry Bounce," Colonial, (C); "Orlinda," Colonial, (B). Note: "Mirror Image" also found on Piecrust shape with light green leaves.

Top row, left to right: "Strathmoor," Colonial, (C); Carol's Roses, Colonial, (B). Middle row, left to right: "Beth," Colonial, (B); "Remembrance," Colonial, (B). Bottom row, left to right: "Iris Ann," Colonial, (B); "Cherish," Colonial, (C).

Top row, left to right: "Deep Green," Colonial, (C); "Apple Butter," Colonial (C). Middle row, left to right: "Maytime," Colonial, (B); "Brookneal," Colonial, (C). Bottom row, left to right: "Mexicano," Astor, (B); "Delta Daisy," Colonial, (B).

Top row, "Pomona" hdl. cake plate. Middle row, left to right: Provincial Farm Scenes Series, 6″ square "Harvester." (B); "Tiger Rag" cake plate (B); "Plowman" (B). Bottom row, left to right: #8 County Fair salad plate, "Pretty in Pink," Colonial, (B); "Thompson Grape," Colonial, (C).

Various square and almost-square plates were made and patterned to go with whatever style or shape of dinnerware the customer wanted. Shown are: Top row, left to right: "Piedmont Plaid," "High Stepper," "Muriel," all (B). Middle row, left to right: "Cradle," "Madras," "Sowing Seed," all (B). Bottom row, left to right: "Grandfather's Clock," "Wren," "Fisherman," all (B). Note: the bottom row and the "Cradle" pattern are parts of the "Country Life" set.

Top row, left to right: "Hilda" gravy tray, Astor, (B); "Hilda" gravy tray, Candlewick, (B); "Caladium" celery, Skyline, (B). Middle row, left to right: "Signal Flags" sherbet, Piecrust, (C); "Becky" eggcup (B); Clinchfield Railway Ashtray, (B); "Chanticleer" sherbet, Skyline, (B). Bottom row, left to right: "Whirligig" open sugar and creamer, Colonial, (B); "Fruit Salad" smaller open sugar and creamer, Colonial (B).

Top row, left to right: "Julie," pie baker; "Dreambirds," Colonial, (B). Middle row, left to right: "Cross Stitch" divided plate; "Butterfly & Leaves," Trellis, (B). Bottom row, center: "Red Bank," tray for waffle set which consists of a covered batter jug and covered syrup jug resting on the tray.

Kitchenware: Top row, left to right, "Petunia" leftover, 6″ dia. x 4¼″ (also found in 4″ and 5″ sizes that stack). "Leaf" syrup jug without lid, 5″ tall , 6 oz; "Tulip" batter pitcher, 7½″ tall, 60 oz. (See tray on page 115). Middle row, left to right: "Rock Rose" divided baker (also with no divisions and chrome holder); "Leaf" lifter, "Cherries" fork and spoon. Bottom row, left to right: "Leaf" covered casserole, 7″ dia., 1 qt.; Happy Home casserole, 8″ dia.

Top row, left to right: "Flower Children" child's feeding dish; "Tutti-Frutti" jumbo cup & saucer; "Twig" shakers. Middle row, left to right: "Leaf" 3 x 3½" Custard; Prairie Rose heavy divided plate, 10"; Sq. 4" tile (tiles also found in 3", 4" & 6" round and square). Bottom row, left to right: Garden Green 4¾" dia. covered Ramekin (also found in larger sizes); 6" sq. tile, Apple ashtray with rests.

Accessory Pieces and Chinaware

Around 1945, a line of about 40 pieces of fine quality vitreous chinaware was introduced. This quality china will be found with either the script mark or the #6 circle mark with the addition of the word "china." Small items will be marked simply "Blue Ridge China." Shakers in the china line are often not marked at all, but have been found in their original blue printed boxes. This was a fairly expensive line for the times and was composed mainly of specialty items such as decorative pitchers, shakers, fancy creamers and sugars, chocolate pots, teapots, vases, fancy relishes and character jugs. You will find items in the same shapes done in both china and regular quality earthenware, such as the Betsy jug, so watch your markings. Except for the shakers, we have found all chinaware is marked. Dinnerware sets were not made in china.

Teapots were made in earthenware decorated to match dinnerware sets and also in china with individual decorations.

Back row, left to right: "Mickey," Colonial, (B); "Windflower," Colonial, (B). Front row, left to right: "Rose Bouquet," China, Snub-nose shape #13/2; "Emalee," demi-pot, (B); "Grape Wine," china, Snub-nose shape.

Top row, left to right: "Bluebell Bouquet," (B), Ball shape; "Tucker," china, Mini-Ball shape; "Glamour," Ball shape, (B). Middle row, left to right: "Green Briar," Piecrust, (B); "Fairmede Fruits," Square Round, (B). Bottom row, left to right: "Susan," Skyline, (B); "Spiderweb," Skyline, (C). Note: Square Round teapots may be found in two sizes: 7″ holding 56 ounces and 6″ holding 40 oz. Skyline pots may also be found in two sizes. "Tucker" teapot carries the Good Housekeeping jobber marking.

Top back: Autumn Apple coffee pot, Ovide shape, (B). Front, left to right: "Good Housekeeping Rose," china, Good Housekeeping shape; "Yellow Rose," china, Chevron Handle shape; and "Lorraine," china, Fine Panel shape. Note: Good Housekeeping was a mark used by Promotions, Inc., Youngstown, OH, 1941 – 43. A matching sugar and creamer will also be found with this backstamp.

Chocolate pots were made in china but sometimes decorated to match earthenware sets. These were sold in their own white gift box. Pictured are, left to right: "Easter Parade," "Rose Marie," "French Peasant," "Chintz."

Some of these pots have been found containing a factory-originated flyer stating "I am a Chocolate Pot." Others have been found marked on the bottom, "Teapot #1." Still, the tray designed to hold the chocolate pot and the pedestal sugar and creamer is often marked "Chocolate #1." But who uses sugar and cream with hot chocolate? I think this is destined to be one of our little mysteries.

Pictured are, back row, left to right: "Whig Rose," Rebecca shape, 8¾", china; "Eunice," Watauga shape, 5¼"; "Chintz," Milady shape, 8¼", china. Front, left to right: Antique #1, 5", china; "Golden Age," Virginia shape, 6½", china; Virginia Jug #2, 6½", china; "Tralee Rose," Spiral shape, 7" Earthenware.

Fancy pitchers were a popular item, and Southern Potteries made a number of them in both china and earthenware. Again, watch your markings. China pitchers often have the shape name incorporated into the backstamp such as Jane, Sally, etc. A number of these molds are currently owned by Clinchfield Artware Pottery and are in production. Size and quality of decoration vary enough from Southern Potteries so that they are easy for a collector to recognize, with the Clinchfield Artware product being larger and the painting more simplistic. Also, Clinchfield Artware Pottery marks their entire production.

Back row, left to right: 7" Abby Jug, decoration #1, china; 9" "Prim" carafe; 7½" "Sculptured Fruit," china (Note: "Sculptured Fruit" comes in three sizes; 7½" holding 52 ounces, 7" holding 40 ounces and 6⅝" holding 32 ounces and sometimes marked Petite Jug). Front row, left to right: 7½" Jane shape, "Scatter" pattern, china; 6" Chick, floral pattern, china; 8¾" Betsy, china (also found in earthenware); 5¾" Grace shape, "Big Blossom" pattern, china. Note: Betsy will be found with various decoration styles. She was made first in earthenware and then in china. Earthenware Betsy will be heavier, slightly smaller than the china pieces, spray or airbrush decorated, sometimes gold decorated and seldom marked.

Top row, left to right: Grace shape, Cobalt splatter, china; Grace shape, plain rose color, earthenware. (Note: Grace will be found in several different plain colors.) 5½″ Clara shape, Nove Rose pattern, china. Middle row, left to right: 4¼″ Spiral shape, "Pansy" pattern, china; 6¼″ Alice shape, "Fairmede Fruits" pattern, earthenware; 4½″ Virginia shape, "Candied Fruit," china. Bottom row, left to right: Antique #1, china; Helen shape, "Grapes" pattern, china; Grace Jug #1, china. (Note: Alice shape will be found in 6″ china also.)

Several fancy vases were produced by Southern Potteries in both china and earthenware. Top row, left to right: 7¾" "Mum Spray," china; 5½" "Hibiscus," china; 7¾" "Tafoya Tulip," china. Middle row, left to right: "Mood Indigo," china; 8" "Gladys" Boot, (B). Bottom row, left to right: 9¼" "Delphine," china; two bud vases (may be more shapes); 9¼" "Flo," china. Note: China vase with "Mood Indigo" pattern also will be found in solid pearlized blue with the old Clinchfield mark.

Top row, left to right: "Augusta," Vanity Fair marked 10″ lamp; "Diamond Lil" American Home marked 10¾″ lamp; "Dogtooth Violet" 7¾″ vase. Middle row, left to right: Charm House 4″ shakers, bonbon tray. Bottom row, left to right: Charm House 7¾″ x 5¼″ handled Marmite with lid; Creamer, Cov. Sugar. Note: Charm House was mark used by China & Glass Distributors Inc., New York, about 1947.

Top row, left to right: Flat Shell or Dorothy Bon-bons "Pixie" and "Palace." (Palace may be found with "Your Gift from the Palace" backstamp). Middle row, left to right: "Evalina," "Nove Rose," both china. Bottom row: "French Knots," Palisades shape relish.

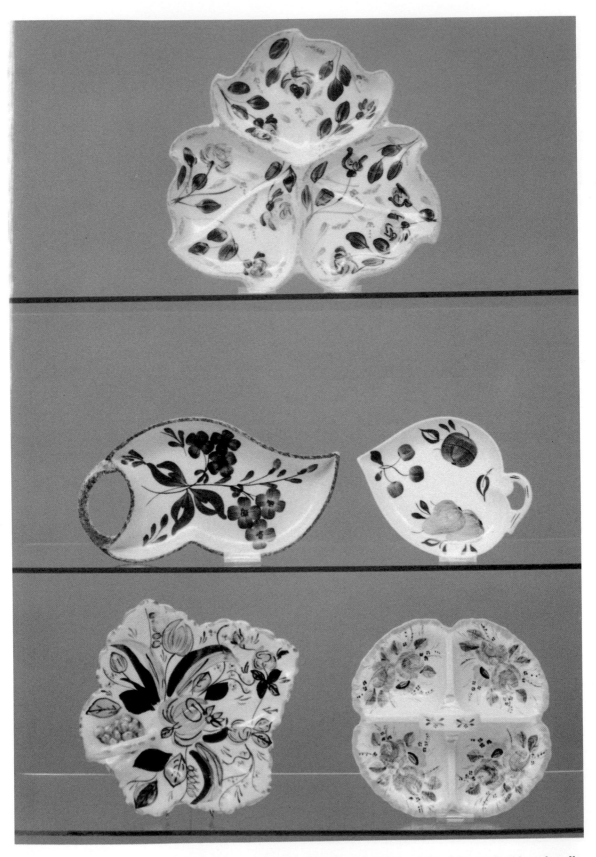

Top row, center: "Rose Parade," Martha snack tray. Middle row, left to right: "Serenade," loop handle, china; "Candied Fruit," loop handle, china. Bottom row, left to right: "Verna" Maple Leaf china cake tray; "Ellen" top handle, four section relish, china.

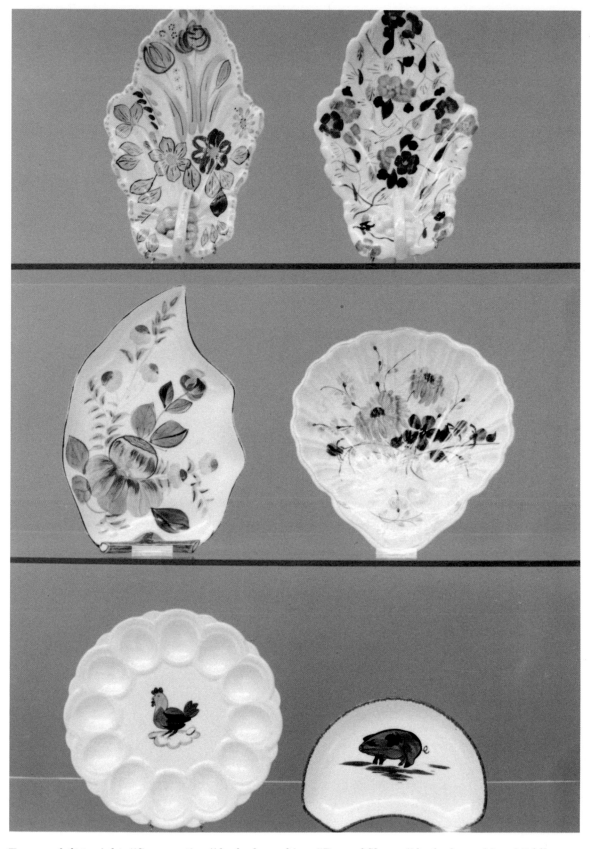

Top row, left to right: "Summertime" leaf celery, china; "Rose of Sharon" leaf celery, china. Middle row, left to right: "Rose Garden" mod leaf, china; "Tussie Mussie," deep shell, china. Bottom row, left to right: "Rooster" egg plate, (C); "Piggie" individual relish.

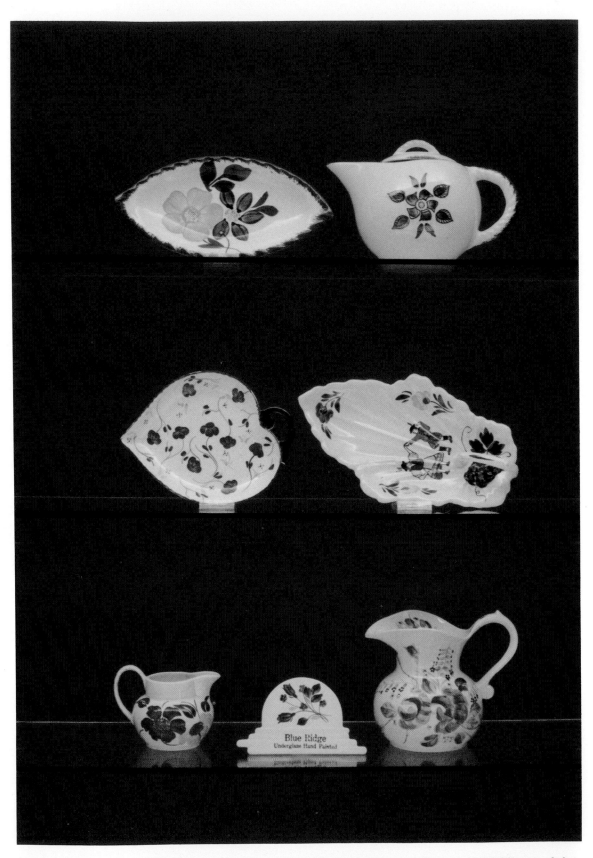

Top row, left to right: Green Briar celery tray; "Half Penney" Rope Handle teapot. Middle row, left to right: Buttons & Forget-Me-Nots heart-shape relish, china; "Swiss Dancers," leaf celery, china. Bottom row, left to right: "Melody" Antique shape pitcher; Blue Ridge counter sign, "Ida Rose" pitcher, Sally shape, china.

China shakers came in their own box and interestingly enough, the box is often all that was marked. The shakers themselves are not always marked. They were decorated by combining elements from many Blue Ridge patterns so that they would "go with" most any pattern the customer selected. Shown are six different patterns in the 5½" china shakers. (For reference, number patterns one through six from left to right, beginning in the foreground.)

Left to right, top to bottom: 6" round candy boxes were produced in many patterns both in china and regular earthenware. Pictured are "Hazel," "Katharine" and "Peacock" all in china. 4¼" square cigarette boxes also were made in many patterns in earthenware. Shown are "Pink Daisy" and "Rooster." The 5¼" covered powder box is elusive; generally made in china. In the foreground are the 3⅛" ashtrays "Butterfly" and "Rooster," They came in a set of four with the cigarette box.

A number of novelty shakers were made in the regular quality earthenware. Top row, left to right: 5¼″ "Blossom Top," 6″ "Bud Top." (Note: Blossom Top will also be found with floral patterns painted on body. Both "Bud Top" and "Blossom Top" were sold as shown.) Next row: "Mallard" (Male 4″, Female 3½″), small "Painted Apples" and "Chickens" (rooster 4¾″, hen 4″). Bottom row: Chickens were made in many painting patterns and colors. "Daisy Chain" range shakers. Note: Apples will be found in small and large sizes, painted solid red or white with various designs.

Several interesting sculptured boxes have been found in the chinaware. Generally used for candy or cigarettes, these are among the few items made by Southern Potteries with raised or sculptured designs. Rear: "Mallard," 5½″x4¼″, china. Center, left to right: "Seaside," 3½″x4½″, china; "Rose Step," 4¼″x5½″, china. Foreground: "Dancing Nude," 4″ china.

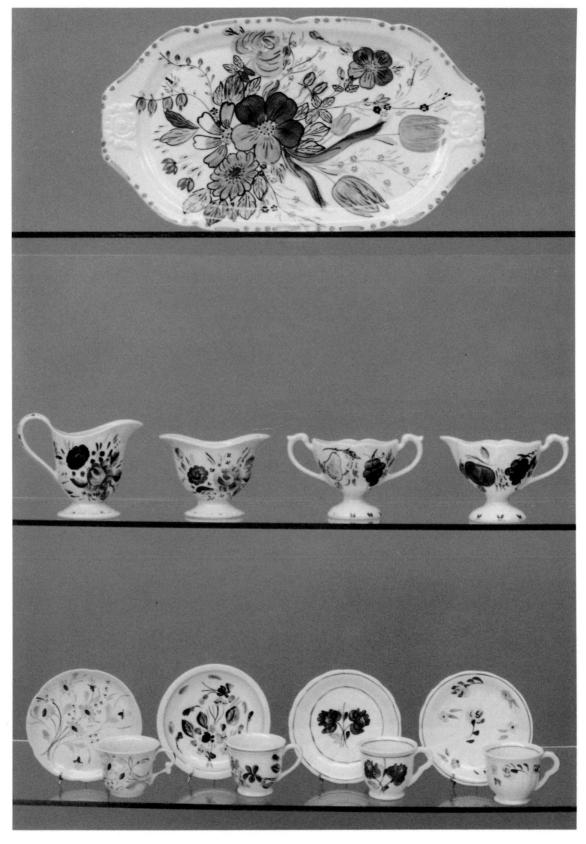

Top row, center: "Elegance" 9 x 15½" chocolate set tray. Middle row, left to right: "Nora" flared sugar and creamer, china. (These are the china demi sugar and creamer.) "Fruit Basket" pedestal sugar and creamer, china. Bottom row, left to right: Demitasse cups and saucers: "Magic Carpet:, china, (A); "Spring Shower," "Rosy Future," "Snippet," (B).

Top row, left to right: China demitasse set, "Spring Bouquet." Middle row, Demi sugar, tray and creamer, Colonial (5½" x 7" tray), "Romance." Bottom row, "Yellow Nocturne" demi creamer, tray and teapot, Skyline shape tray (9½" x 7⅝").

Southern Potteries was known through the years for its extremely diversified manufacturing and sales programs. Outlets were found not only for first quality ware, but seconds and sometimes even thirds. Occasionally, you will find pieces of the Blue Ridge with aluminum edgings, overhandles, etc. Various specialty houses or jobbers would purchase items from Southern Potteries (often seconds) and apply the metal parts, reselling the resulting piece to various retail shops. Tiered tid bits and center-handle servers using both metal and wooden handles fall into this same category. The jobber drilled the plates and assembled the servers themselves.

Pictured are: Aluminum-edged 10" basket in "Whirligig" pattern and 7" basket in "Red Flower." Center handle server, 10¼" in "Mountain Cherry," Candlewick; Three-tier tidbit (5½", 7½", 10½") in "Apple and Pear," Woodcrest.

Possibly the most sought-after of the boxes is the "Sherman Lily Box." Found with various paintings on lid and sides, shown here in "Dimity" pattern. Mortality rate was high on the lovely, formed and applied lily and lucky is the collector who owns one of these rare boxes.

Top row, left to right: "Miss Mouse" plate, Skyline, (B); "Duck in Hat" feeding dish, "Humpty" cereal, Skyline, (B). Middle row, left to right: Circus set, plate, mug, cereal bowl. Bottom row, left to right: "Bunny Hop" plate, Skyline, (B); "Pig & Pals," divided feeder. Note: "Bunny Hop" may also be found in blue and has a matching mug.

"Square Dance" party set (B). Note: each plate is different in decoration while cups are decorated alike. Also found with this decoration in Colonial are a 14″ plate, 11½″ bowl and 7½″ square plates.

"County Fair," Colonial, (B). In 1941, Avon Products Inc., gave a set of eight of these 8½″ salad plates to salespeople who managed to send in single orders of $150.00-199.00. These and other salad plate sets were quite popular and came in a number of different patterns with each plate bearing a different pattern, but tied together by central theme or border treatments. Shown are seven of the eight Avon premium plates. For reference, number one through seven, left to right, starting at top row. You will find matching cups and saucers, serving or chop plate and 6″ square plates in this pattern, also with a red edge instead of green. Keep in mind, however, that only the 8½″ plates were used by Avon for their premium. "County Fair" plates also found with red borders, and in 6″ square plates. For eighth plate, see page 112.

Salad set: "Songbirds" Astor. Shown are seven of eight designs.

Salad set: "Duff" on Candlewick. Shown are seven of eight designs. "Duff" sets will also be found with green swirled background. Eighth plate is set has single pear with one green leaf.

Salad Sets: Shown are partial sets. Top row: "Honolulu," Candlewick, #1 and #2. Middle row, left to right: "Banded Fruit," Candlewick, #1 and #2. Bottom row, left to right: "Banded Fruit," Candlewick, #3 and #4.

Partial Salad Sets: Top row, left to right: "Lavender Fruit," Colonial, (C); "Astor Fruit," Astor, (B). Middle row, left to right: "Language of Flowers," Candlewick, (B); "Cherries Jubilee," Colonial, (B). Bottom row, left to right: "Fruit Cocktail," Astor, #1 and #2, (B).

Salad Set: "Garden Flowers," Colonial, (B). Top row, left to right: "Kansas Gayfeather," "Red Cone Flower," "Hollyhock." Middle row, left to right: "Lavender Iris," "Yellow Pansy," "Blue Morning Glory." Bottom row, left to right: "Yellow Mums," "Single Poinsetta."

Salad set - Skyline Birds. Top row, left to right: Yellow-shafted Flicker, Hooded Warbler, Scrub or Florida Jay. Middle row, left to right: Ivory-billed Woodpecker, Catbird, Hummingbird. Bottom row, left to right: Summer Tanager, Oriole.

Top row, Colonial Birds salad plates #3, #4, #5, Colonial (B). Middle row, left to right: "Jubilee Fruit" salad plate #1, Colonial (B). Colonial Birds salad plate #6, Colonial (B). Bottom row, left to right: "Jubilee Fruits" salad plates #2, #3, #4 Colonial (B).

The premium trade was not forgotten. In 1953, Quaker Oats offered a four-piece set consisting of a cup, saucer, cereal bowl and plate decorated with a single red apple and three green leaves done on the Candlewick blank. Customers sent to "Box Q, Erwin, Tennessee" for their premium. Pictured is the set with original mailing box. (Photo by Bill Newbound). Note: Large plates and platters will be found with two apples.

At the 1985 Blue Ridge Show in Erwin, TN, these 11½″ Specialty Plates turned up. They are on the Candlewick shape, although the central "Big Catch" pattern has also been found on a Clinchfield shape platter. Done in shades of blue. (See cover, Book II). They are not artist signed, but evidently are in short supply. They are: left to right - "Bird Dog," "Big Catch" and "Fala," the latter being named after the famous little Scottie that shared the White House with President Franklin Roosevelt. The number painted and the exact time period of manufacture remains a mystery.

Stanley Home Products ordered a set of Ivy decorated dinnerware as a hostess gift or premium for having a Stanley home party. This was about 1947. Pieces were marked Stanhome. (See Marks section).

Blue Ridge items were also offered by leading trading stamp companies and, in the mid-1950's, some Montgomery Ward stores gave a set of Blue Ridge dinnerware as a gift with the purchase of a dinette set. A number of supermarkets gave their customers Blue Ridge dishes with a certain amount in grocery purchases. Customers could then purchase extra pieces from the store for a nominal sum. (See Rope Handle shape).

Searching for methods to enable them to stay afloat in a declining market, Southern Potteries, in the mid-1950's, produced a line of hand-decorated table lamp bases which they sold to lamp manufacturers. The handled vase was one mold used for this purpose. The vase section of the lamp will be somewhat larger than the original chinaware vase. Lamps have been found marked "Vanity Fair" and "Family Guild Genuine Porcelain." Lamps made from coffee and teapots, and wall sconces made from plates and cups and saucers have turned up, but we believe the bulk of these to be of recent manufacture.

Also, at the time of closing, Southern Potteries had developed a line of ceramic building tile. These were much larger than the conventional one-inch and four-inch kitchen, bath, and institutional type tile, measuring nine or ten inches by twelve to fifteen inches. These were to be made in both flat and corner shapes and also in windowsill sizes. However, quite a bit of retooling and kiln adaptation was required in manufacture and I do not believe they were marketed to any extent, if at all.

Reproductions

In 1985-86, a few reproduction Character Jugs surfaced at various markets. They bore a #6 backstamp on the base, but were in earthenware rather than porcelain. A flurry of vases, pitchers and teapots followed, mainly in shapes that were never made by Southern Potteries except for the Rebecca and Milday jug shapes. Generally, the painting on these pieces was inferior to that of the Southern Potteries originals, and in size they are somewhat larger.

To identify a reproduction Character Jug, examine the inside of the jug where the handle attaches to the main body. If there is a hole, top and/or bottom indicating that the handle is molded in one with the body, you have a reproduction. The original porcelain jug handles were attached or applied, keeping the inside of the jug smooth.

After the reproductions were exposed, other pieces began to show up bearing a backstamp with the words "Original Blue Ridge Pattern, SPI, Erwin Pottery," so check your marks carefully before you purchase. (See mark below.)

Character Jugs

In the mid-1950's, a line of china character jugs was introduced. They were an expensive line for the times and not made in large numbers. The quality of workmanship in both mold making and decorating is outstanding. The faces have personality and are the cream-of-the-crop in any Blue Ridge collection. Included in the line were the Pioneer Woman (6½" tall), Daniel Boone (6" tall), Paul Revere (6¼" tall) and the Indian (6¾" tall). All but the Indian have their name incised in the base. Why the Indian was left out is a mystery. The marked jugs we have in our collection all bear the #6 mark with the addition of the word "china." Following Southern Potteries usual hit-and-miss marking methods, not all jugs will be marked. This has no significance; they just simply missed being stamped.

The molds for these jugs now belong to the Clinchfield Artware Pottery owned by the Cash Family in Erwin, Tennessee, and are in production intermittently. The Clinchfield Artware Pottery jugs all bear the Cash family's own marking. Also, due to the great difference in the materials used for the bodies, the Clinchfield Artware Pottery jugs do not shrink during firing to the extent that the Southern Potteries china jugs did, making their overall dimensions noticeably larger. The quality and painting does not compare with that of Southern Potteries and should not confuse knowledgable Blue Ridge collectors.

Pictured are: Daniel Boone, Pioneer Woman, Paul Revere and Indian. Notice the tomahawk handle on the Indian and Daniel's coonskin-tail handle.

Artist Signed Pieces

During the mid-1940's, a few of the very best decorators from Southern Potteries were selected to do a limited number of scenic and wildlife plates and large platters. They are signed with the artist's name on the lower right hand edge, or sometimes the lower center edge of the painting. The artists we have discovered thus far are: Frances Kyker (Treadway), Mae Garland (Hice), Ruby S. Hart, Nelsene Q. Calhoun, Mildred Broyles, Alleene Miller, Louise Guinn and Mildred Banner (Ed-wards). These unusually beautiful plates and platters are fine examples of true American folk art that should be preserved and treasured. Surely they are the ultimate in any Blue Ridge collection. Oddly enough, these pieces were not done on china blanks, but on the regular quality earthenware. The "Quail" plate is done on the Colonial blank, while the "Turkey" platters and "Cabin" and "Mill" plates used the old Clinchfield blank. All pieces shown are marked with the #4 script mark.

Pictured are: "Quail" plate, Colonial blank, 11¾", signed Frances Kyker; "Flower Cabin" plate, Clinchfield blank, 10½", signed Frances Kyker.

"White Mill" 10½″ plate, Clinchfield, signed Nelsene Q. Calhoun. Photo by Bryce London.

"Green Mill" 10½″ plate, Clinchfield, signed Ruby S. Hart. Photo by Bill Newbound.

"Gold Cabin" 10½″ plate, Clinchfield, signed Nelsene Q. Calhoun. Photo by Bill Newbound.

"Turkey Gobbler" 17½″ platter, Clinchfield, signed Mae Garland. Also found in dinner plate size and, very rarely, in cups and saucers.

"Wild Turkey" 17½" platter, signed Mae Garland.

United Wallpaper Company, makers of Talisman Wallpapers, had offices located in the Merchandise Mart in Chicago, just one floor above the Southern Potteries offices. In approximately 1950-1952, an idea was formulated to produce several coordinated wallpaper and chinaware patterns. This idea was put into operation on a small scale, but did not prove successful and was abandoned after a short period. Pictured is an advertising or counter plate. This shape plate has also been found advertising Primrose China (a jobber) and Blue Ridge dinnerware.

Talisman Wallpaper Ads

Cherry Time

Woodbine

Talisman Wild Strawberry

See also Yorktown (page 96) and Blossom Tree (page 70).

Clinchfield Ware

When Southern Potteries was first established in 1916-1917, the product was known as Clinchfield Ware or Clinchfield China. A 1930's ad proclaimed, "Clinchfield on China is like Sterling on Silver." Decoration was decal, gold lining and trim. The bulk of this dinnerware is of little interest to the collector since it does not vary that much from the output of any of the hundreds of other potteries operating at that time. However, there are facets of the production that can make a nice addition to the Blue Ridge collection. Some of the decal decorated pieces were quite elaborate with wide, richly colored borders covered with gold lace surrounding the central motif. Often these will carry the interesting Brotherhood of Operative Potters mark on the reverse side. Or you may find what Southern called "Souvenir Plaques" which were plates with an advertising or a special order message such as Christmas greetings on either side. These were made for businesses, individuals, or organizations. The buttermilk pitcher was popular for many years and much copied by other potteries, while the "Bluebird" dinnerware is avidly hunted by "Bluebird" china collectors countrywide.

Sometime prior to 1932-33, Southern Potteries made a line of large animal figures including elephants, lions, tigers, dogs, cats, rabbits and penguins. So far, only a very few marked examples of these figures have surfaced. Almost all potteries made animal figures and were not averse to copying from each other, so unless you stumble onto a marked piece, animal figures are impossible to authenticate. A few figural flower holders featuring lovely Art Nouveau type ladies have been found, but again unless they are marked, it is impossible to authenticate them as being a Southern Potteries product. Some of the early pieces were covered entirely in an orangy lustre or a pearlized finish looking almost Japanese. We have seen the handled vase decorated in this manner.

If you decide to collect Clinchfield items, do study carefully the marks section. Keep in mind that the Cash Family Pottery uses marks that include the words "Clinchfield Art Ware" and "Blue Ridge." If the words "Art" or "Cash Family" appear in a mark, the product is not by Southern Potteries.

Matching Glassware

Glass tumblers, juices, and dessert cups painted to match Blue Ridge patterns were available during the late 1940's, mainly from Montgomery Ward and Sears Roebuck. During the mid-1940's, Earl Newton and Associates were Chicago representatives for both Southern Potteries and Imperial Glass Company. Mr. Newton also operated a small glass factory in Bowling Green, Ohio. Working as he did in both the glass and chinaware fields, Mr. Newton conceived the idea of matching glassware to Blue Ridge patterns. He sent his decorator to Southern Potteries to learn some of the Blue Ridge patterns and techniques and began producing the matching glassware. The idea proved quite successful, especially with Montgomery Ward who purchased the main bulk of the factory output, and to a lesser extent with Sears Roebuck & Company.

After awhile, Mr. Newton began augmenting his supply of glass with the purchase of various shapes and sizes of blanks from Libbey Glass in Ohio and sometimes from Federal Glass Company. Various sizes of tumblers were also decorated on a frosted background instead of clear.

The main pieces available were: 12 oz. tumblers, 5 oz. juices, and dessert cups. Advertisements have been found for matching glassware in the following patterns:

Ridge Daisy	Petal Point	Ridge Harvest	Mountain Ivy
Sun Bouquet	Green Briar	Crab Apple	Cumberland

Sets You Can Collect

The following listings are examples of advertised dinnerware and specialty sets. Keep in mind that Southern Potteries was very flexible in its production and put sets together in whatever combinations their customers requested. The demi-sized pieces are a good example. The demi-pot, cup, saucer, sugar and creamer made one set, sometimes with a matching tray, sometimes without. Or, the demi-pot, sugar and creamer added to the regular sized cup and saucer, 6¼" and 8½" plates, covered toast, egg cup, butter pat and cereal bowl made up the Breakfast set.

Twenty-piece Starter Set: 4 each: 9⅜" plate, cup saucer, 6¼" plate, 5¼" fruit.

Ten-piece Cake Set: 4 7½" square plates, 12" square cake plate, cake lifter.

Twelve-piece Salad Set: 8 8½" round salad plate, 10¼" salad bowl, salad fork, salad spoon, 12" serving plate.

Nineteen-piece Party Set: 8 8½" party plates with cup well, 8 cups, 10½" cake plate, small creamer, open sugar (no handles).

Sixteen-piece Child's Set: 4 demi-cups, 4 demi-saucers, 4 6¼" plates, demi-creamer, demi-sugar, 6" demi-pot with lid.

Thirteen-piece Breakfast Set: 8½" plate, 6¼" plate, cup, saucer, covered toast (2 pc.), double egg cup, butter pat, cereal bowl, demi-sugar, demi-creamer, demi-pot with lid (2 pc.).

Getting Help and Finding Friends

Subscribe to: *The National Blue Ridge Newsletter*
Norma Lilly, 144 Highland Dr.
Blountville, TN 37617
  Six issues yearly – $12.00

The Daze
275 S. State Rd., Box 57
Otisville, MI 48463
  Monthly – $19.00

The New Glaze
Box 4782
Birmingham, AL 35206
  Yearly (11 issues) – $12.00

Join: Blue Ridge Collectors Club
c/o Phyllis Ledford
Route 3, Box 161
Erwin, TN 37650
  Meets third Tuesday of each month at Senior Citizens Building, Erwin. Dues – $5.00 year

Visit: Unicoi Heritage Museum (Old Fishery House)
Erwin-Johnson City Hwy., Rts. 19/23
Three Miles from Erwin, TN
  Museum includes two rooms containing Blue Ridge dinnerware. Displays are changed periodically.

National Advertising

Considerable national advertising was done, mainly from about 1940 through 1956. Southern Potteries' ads were found in several of the leading home magazines such as *Better Homes & Gardens, House & Garden, American Home* and *House Beautiful.*

Both Sears Roebuck & Company and Montgomery Ward carried Blue Ridge during this same period. The following pages show examples of catalog pages and national advertising. Look carefully, perhaps you will find your pattern here.

House & Garden, 1948

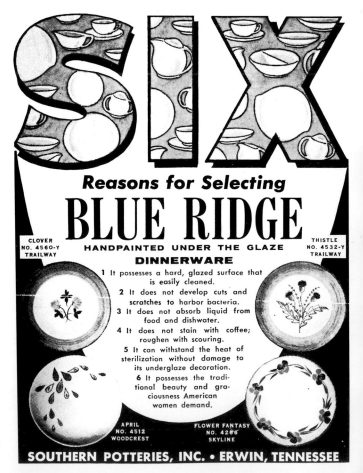

Lastingly Lovely
PIE CRUST DINNERWARE
by Blue Ridge

DIXIE HARVEST (No. 3913) is another outstanding pattern on our new Pie Crust shape. Its exotic beauty is permanently sealed Under the Glaze and every piece a Hand Painted original creation, yet modestly priced.

Blue Ridge DINNERWARE
SOUTHERN POTTERIES, INC.

House Beautiful, December, 1954

SIX
Reasons for Selecting
BLUE RIDGE
HANDPAINTED UNDER THE GLAZE
DINNERWARE

CLOVER NO. 4560-Y TRAILWAY

THISTLE NO. 4532-Y TRAILWAY

1 It possesses a hard, glazed surface that is easily cleaned.
2 It does not develop cuts and scratches to harbor bacteria.
3 It does not absorb liquid from food and dishwater.
4 It does not stain with coffee; roughen with scouring.
5 It can withstand the heat of sterilization without damage to its underglaze decoration.
6 It possesses the traditional beauty and graciousness American women demand.

APRIL NO. 4512 WOODCREST

FLOWER FANTASY NO. 4286 SKYLINE

SOUTHERN POTTERIES, INC. • ERWIN, TENNESSEE

Marks

In the beginning, approximately 1917-1923, Southern Potteries produced decal decorated dinnerware under the name Clinchfield Ware or Clinchfield China Ware. These pieces carried the Clinchfield markings, in circles with or without a crown, and in block letters as shown.

Following the Clinchfield marks were the three Southern Potteries marks. These are not necessarily in order of use:

#1   #2   #3

The name "Blue Ridge" was introduced about 1932 or 1933. Since any surviving company records have long since vanished, and the memories of those who worked with marks at Southern Potteries are fading with the years, we cannot give any firm dates as to when various marks were used. In fact, there were periods when several marks were obviously used at the same time. We know the "Blue Ridge China" (#5) mark was used after 1945 because that is when china production began. Also, it is safe to say that the marks bearing the words "detergent proof" and "oven safe" (#7, #8, #9) were used in the late years. We will show the various marks in the approximate order in which our detective work has placed them, but we must ask you to remember that marks were used concurrently.

The marks most often found are the #4 script marking and the very familiar #6 circle mark using the Blue Ridge Mountains motif with the Lonesome Pine in the foreground. (Remember the "Trail of the Lonesome Pine"?)

We are numbering the most often found Blue Ridge marks for your convenience. Also, we are showing drawings of several "occasionally found" Blue Ridge marks that were used on short lines of production or during the transition period from decal to hand painting.

Blue Ridge
Hand Painted
Underglaze
Southern Potteries, Inc.
MADE IN U. S. A.
10D

#4

Blue Ridge
China
Hand Painted
Underglaze
Southern Potteries, Inc.
MADE IN U. S. A.

#5

#6

#7   #8   #9

Occasionally Found and Jobber Marks

You will find many pieces that look like Blue Ridge but have different markings. Southern Potteries was a very large concern and worked for many different jobbers including supermarkets and trading stamp companies. These jobbers were mainly smaller companies who occasionally sold wholesale and sometimes retail to their own clientele. They ordered stock from Southern Potteries and often wanted these pieces backstamped with their own marks. Some of the patterns used were exclusive to the jobber and some were regular Blue Ridge patterns. That is why you will sometimes find two plates with the identical pattern, one bearing a Blue Ridge mark and one having a jobber mark. About 1947, for instance, Stanley Home Products chose a Southern Potteries dinnerware set to be given as a hostess gift or premium for having a Stanley Home Party. These pieces were marked with the Stanhome backstamp. Cannonsburg Pottery continued this "Stanhome Ivy" pattern after Southern closed, so some pieces will be found with the Cannonsburg mark.

Since none of the Southern Potteries patterns were copyrighted, they were prey to pattern thievery. Several companies copied Blue Ridge patterns. In one case, a jobber even took several popular patterns to Japan and had them reproduced into dinnerware made in that country!

Besides the marks illustrated, other jobber marks or backstamps you may find include: "Westfall China Company," "PLC Colonial Faience USA," and "Primrose China."

Jobber Marks

Ucagco
Underglaze
Hand Painted
U.S.A.

Good Housekeeping
Genuine China

NASCO
Underglaze
Hand Painted
MADE IN
U.S.A.

Charm House
FINE CHINA — C G — HAND PAINTED

P.V.

FONDEVILLE
NEW YORK

Mount Vernon
Hand Painted
UNDERGLAZE
MADE IN U.S.A.

KING'S
HAND PAINTED
UNDERGLAZE
MADE IN U.S.A.

Etc.

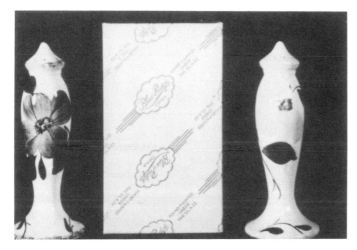

China shakers often came in this attractive light blue box with "Blue Ridge China, Hand Painted Under the Glaze" printed in dark blue.

Southern Potteries building showing the original old beehive kilns.

Southern Potteries warehouse - can you find your pattern? Notice wall in back of room that is hung with hundreds of sample plates.

Index

Price Guide

I cannot emphasize too strongly that this is a price GUIDE, not to be looked upon as the ultimate final word! As with any collectible, prices will vary from one part of the country to another. Keep in mind that Blue Ridge is a new collectible and prices suggested are an average for this moment in time. As Blue Ridge becomes established and firm patterns of supply and demand are discovered, there will necessarily be fluctuations in pricing.

In the 1942 – 43 catalog from Sears Roebuck & Company's 1942-43 catalog, the descriptive text for Blue Ridge dinnerware contained this statement: "The more colors and greater amount of handwork in the design, the more expensive the pattern." This still makes a lot of sense to me, as some Blue Ridge patterns contain perhaps one motif in contrast to others that are covered with elaborate designs. In a few instances, even though the pattern itself is a fairly simple one, it has an appeal that will place it in a little higher category pricewise.

All these factors are the reason we are using A–B–C pricing scale as follows:

A – China, Artist-Signed and rare

B – Elaborate and appealing patterns

C – Simple and solid patterns

Under each picture in the pattern section, you will find a pattern name, a shape name and a price guide letter. This letter indicates the suggested pricing category.

In general, prices will be higher for patterns depicting people (as in French Peasant), birds, animals or fowl. Also, keep in mind that prices are usually higher close to the place of original manufacture. The whole thing boils right down to an article being worth "just what somebody will pay for it." Note: Prices for "French Peasant" type patterns will be perhaps 100% more than shown in following price listings.

A – China, Artist-Signed and rare   B – Elaborate and appealing patterns   C – Simple and solid patterns

N/A denotes price not available.

	(A)	(B)	(C)		(A)	(B)	(C)
Ashtrays, individual	12.00 – 15.00	10.00 – 14.00	8.00 – 10.00	Bon-Bon, divided, ctr. handle	75.00 – 90.00		
Ashtrays, with rest		15.00 – 18.00		Bon-Bon, flat shell	50.00 – 65.00		
Ashtrays, advertising	50.00 – 75.00			Bowl, 5¼" fruit		3.00 – 5.00	2.00 – 4.00

	(A)	(B)	(C)
Bowl, 6" cereal/soup		7.00 – 10.00	4.00 – 6.00
Bowl, 8" flat soup		12.00 – 15.00	8.00 – 10.00
Bowl, 10½" salad		45.00 – 50.00	30.00 – 35.00
Bowl, 11½" salad "Square Dancers"		80.00 – 90.00	
Bowl, covered vegetable		50.00 – 70.00	35.00 – 40.00
Bowl, 8½" mixing		25.00 – 35.00	
Bowl, 8" round vegetable		12.00 – 17.00	8.00 – 10.00
Bowl, 8" round div. veg.		18.00 – 25.00	10.00 – 15.00
Bowl, 9" oval vegetable		18.00 – 20.00	10.00 – 15.00
Bowl, 9" oval div. veg.		25.00 – 29.00	15.00 – 20.00
Box, 6" round covered candy	90.00 –100.00		
Box, Cigarette		65.00 – 75.00	
Box, Dancing Nudes	250.00 –350.00		
Box, Mallard	450.00 –500.00		
Box, round cov. powder	95.00 –125.00		
Box, Rose Step	90.00 –100.00		
Box, Seaside	90.00 –100.00		
Box, Sherman Lily	500.00 –650.00		
Breakfast Set		350.00 –375.00	
Butterdish		35.00 – 45.00	25.00 – 35.00
Butter Pat/Coaster		25.00 – 30.00	10.00 – 15.00
Cake Lifter		20.00 – 25.00	
Cake Tray, Maple Leaf	45.00 – 55.00		
Carafe, with lid		55.00 – 60.00	
Casserole, with lid		35.00 – 45.00	
Celery, Leaf Shape	25.00 – 35.00		
Celery, Skyline		25.00 – 30.00	
Child's Cereal		25.00 – 35.00	
Child's Mug		25.00 – 30.00	
Child's Plate		25.00 – 30.00	
Child's Feeding Dish		25.00 – 35.00	
Child's Play Set		250.00 –300.00	
Chocolate Pot	100.00 –175.00		
Chocolate Tray	350.00 –425.00		
Coffee Pot		95.00 –110.00	
Counter Sign	175.00 –200.00		
Creamer, demi	45.00 –60.00	25.00 – 35.00	
Creamer, regular		5.00 – 8.00	3.00 – 6.00
Creamer, china pedestal	40.00 – 60.00		
Cup & Saucer, demi	25.00 – 35.00	20.00 – 25.00	
Cup & Saucer, jumbo		30.00 – 40.00	
Cup & Saucer, regular		8.00 – 10.00	5.00 – 7.00
Cup & Saucer, holiday		35.00 – 40.00	
Custard		9.00 – 15.00	
Dish, 8x13", baking		20.00 – 25.00	
Egg Cup, double		20.00 – 30.00	
Egg Dish, deviled		30.00 – 35.00	
Glass Tumbler		12.00 – 14.00	
Glass Dessert Cup		10.00 – 12.00	
Glass Juice Tumbler		9.00 – 12.00	
Gravy Boat		15.00 – 22.00	10.00 – 14.00
Gravy Tray		20.00 – 25.00	
Jugs, Character	500.00 – 700.00		
Jug, Covered Batter		55.00 – 75.00	
Jug, Covered Syrup		75.00 – 90.00	
Lamp, china	100.00 –135.00		
Lamp, from pitcher, teapot, etc.		65.00 – 75.00	
Lazy Susan, 6 pc. w/tray		550.00 – 600.00	
Pie Baker		25.00 – 30.00	
Pitcher, Abby	75.00 – 85.00	45.00 – 55.00	
Pitcher, Alice	85.00 – 90.00	65.00 – 75.00	
Pitcher, Antique	65.00 – 75.00		
Pitcher, Antique, small	70.00 – 80.00		
Pitcher, Betsy	95.00 – 125.00	75.00 – 90.00	
Pitcher, Chick	80.00 – 95.00		
Pitcher, Clara	70.00 – 85.00		40.00 – 45.00
Pitcher, Grace	70.00 – 85.00	35.00 – 45.00	
Pitcher, Helen	80.00 – 90.00		
Pitcher, Jane	85.00 – 95.00		
Pitcher, Milady	95.00 – 125.00		
Pitcher, Sally	125.00 – 130.00		
Pitcher, Sculptured Fruit	65.00 – 75.00		
Pitcher, Spiral		55.00 – 65.00	
Pitcher, Spiral, small	70.00 – 85.00		

	(A)	(B)	(C)
Pitcher, Rebecca	90.00 – 125.00		
Pitcher, Virginia	65.00 – 75.00		
Pitcher, Virginia, small	75.00 – 85.00		
Pitcher, Watuga	150.00 – 175.00		
Plate, Artist – signed	500.00 – 570.00		
Plate, 12" aluminum edge		20.00 – 25.00	
Plate, 11½"–12"		25.00 – 30.00	
Plate, 10½" cake		25.00 – 30.00	18.00 – 20.00
Plate, 10" dinner		15.00 – 20.00	8.00 – 10.00
Plate, 9½" dinner		12.00 – 15.00	8.00 – 12.00
Plate, 3 – compartment snack		15.00 – 20.00	
Plate, Party with cup well & cup		25.00 – 30.00	20.00 – 22.00
Plate, 6"		3.00 – 5.00	2.50 – 3.00
Plate, 6" square, novelty patterns		40.00 – 45.00	
Plate, 7" pie		8.00 – 10.00	7.00 – 9.00
Plate, 8"		8.00 – 10.00	7.00 – 9.00
Plate, 8½" Bird Salad		55.00 – 65.00	
Plate, Various Salad Set patterns		17.00 – 22.00	12.00 – 15.00
Plate, Language of Flowers		55.00 – 75.00	
Plates, Specialty		95.00 – 125.00	
Plates, Designer		55.00 – 65.00	
Plate, Christmas or Turkey		65.00 – 75.00	
Platter, Artist – signed	800.00 – 900.00		
Platter, Turkey w/Acorns or Thanksgiving		190.00 – 200.00	
Platter, 12½"		12.00 – 15.00	9.00 – 12.00
Platter, 15"		20.00 – 25.00	15.00 – 17.00
Platter, 11"		10.00 – 12.50	7.00 – 9.00
Ramekin, 5" with lid		25.00 – 30.00	
Ramekin, 7½" with lid		25.00 – 35.00	
Relish, deep shell	50.00 – 55.00		
Relish, Loop handle	65.00 – 90.00		
Relish, Heart shape	40.00 – 45.00		
Relish, T-handle	35.00 – 45.00		
Relish, Mod Leaf	55.00 – 65.00		
Salad Fork	30.00 – 35.00	25.00 – 35.00	
Salad Spoon		20.00 – 30.00	
Server, center handle		20.00 – 25.00	
Shakers, Apple, pair		10.00 – 12.00	
Shakers, Blossom Top, pair		30.00 – 35.00	
Shakers, Bud Top, pair		30.00 – 35.00	
Shakers, Chickens, pair		80.00 – 95.00	
Shakers, Mallards, pair		135.00 – 155.00	
Shakers, Tall, ftd, china, pair	45.00 – 50.00		
Shakers, regular short		12.00 – 18.00	
Sherbet		18.00 – 22.00	10.00 – 15.00
Sugar, demi	30.00 – 40.00	25.00 – 30.00	
Sugar, Pedestal	40.00 – 50.00		
Sugar, regular w/lid		12.00 – 15.00	8.00 – 10.00
Sugar, wide, open		15.00 – 20.00	
Tea Tile, 6", round or square		25.00 – 35.00	
Tea Tile, 3", round or square		20.00 – 25.00	
Teapot, Ball shape		45.00 – 50.00	
Teapot, Charm House		100.00 – 150.00	
Teapot, Chevron Handle	85.00 – 90.00		
Teapot, Colonial shape		80.00 – 95.00	
Teapot, Demi	100.00 – 150.00	70.00 – 90.00	
Teapot, Fine Panel	85.00 – 100.00		
Teapot, Good Housekeeping	95.00 – 100.00		
Teapot, Piecrust		75.00 – 95.00	
Teapot, Small Ball	75.00 – 95.00		
Teapot, Snub Nose	95.00 – 110.00		
Teapot, Square Round		70.00 – 75.00	
Teapot, Woodcrest		95.00 – 125.00	
Tidbit, 2 – Tier		20.00 – 25.00	18.00 – 20.00
Tidbit, 3 – Tier		20.00 – 30.00	17.00 – 20.00
Toast, covered		95.00 – 100.00	
Tray, Waffle Set		50.00 – 55.00	
Vase, Bud		75.00 – 90.00	
Vase, 5½" Round	65.00 – 75.00		
Vase, Tapered	75.00 – 90.00		
Vase, Handled	70.00 – 75.00		
Vase, 8" Boot		75.00 – 85.00	
Vase, 9¼" Ruffle Top	80.00 – 90.00		
Wallpaper Adv. Plate		250.00 – 325.00	
Wall Sconce		60.00 – 65.00